You H

God Has a Plan For Me

John A. Ward

DISCLAIMER

I have tried to recreate events, locales and conversations from my memories of them. In order to maintain their anonymity, in some instances I have changed the names of individuals and places. I may have changed some identifying characteristics and details such as physical properties, occupations and places of residence.

If you know you know.

ACKNOWLEDGMENTS

First and foremost, GOD THE ALMIGHTY, THE ALL POWERFUL, THE MOST GENEROUS, my wife Jacky, my kids, Nasia and Kamar. My momz, my popz, grandmother and grandfather, my brothers and sisters, Taki, may god be pleased with him. Kenin, Val, Nadia, Jazzy, Sierra. The Umma of Rasululah (SAW). My brother Kenny Gouch, who inspired me to get the project rolling, gave me the paper to write the book. My addiction to crime, the first step, I admitted the problem. Now I'm over you. The parole panel for denying me. With success, I'll be laughing at yall ass. Again, thank you God.

P.S. Oh yea, shoutouts to Mach, the extra slices of paper helped complete the joint, good looking. Shoutouts to Paco. Cousin E.

LET'S GO

1. TRANSFORMING

I'm Jonathan A. Ward, don't worry about what the A stands for. It's 1984, I'm 11 years old, and my favorite TV show is the Dukes of Hazzard. Me and my older brother Taki used to watch it together. My little brother Kenin was just a kid, so he couldn't hang out with us.

We also had two little sisters, Val and Nadia. Breakdancing was the shit at the time, and I was nice. Mostly at popping. My moms, Adrienne Ward used to enter me and my brother Taki into talent shows in New York.

I'll never forget this big one in Manhattan called 'Talent America.' I swear, this is where the musical cats came from. Anyway I guess I did pretty good at that show. This movie producer wanted me to be in a movie but there was a catch, I had to learn how to tap dance.

You might be thinking that's alright to be in a movie, might get on big, who knows? Just learn how to tap dance. No way. I thought that was for girls, so that's that. What a fool right?

One day while watching our favorite show, my moms demanded that we stop to check out this movie called "Roots". This changed my life forever. I couldn't believe what I was seeing, Kunta Kinte automatically became my new hero. Fuck the Dukes of Hazzard.

When I was in maybe 3rd or 4th grade, I used to like Miss Douglas' creative writing class. She told me on numerous occasions that my stories touched her soul. She really encouraged me although school is going to be a thing of the past for me.

Lionel Strums was from Nelton Court, The projects right next to our apartment building. Light skin tall dude, I didn't like him. He was trying to show off in front of some girl classmates and so he clocked me in the head with these cubbies that we used to hold our books and other classroom materials.

After I thrashed him, I ran out of school straight home. My mom's boyfriend's name was Keith Fly. He used to send me downstairs in the building on the first floor to cop him a dime bag of smoke. Back then, they served the dime bag in manila envelope packages, and they were stuffed. The Rastas always served me. All I had to say was, Keith wants a dime. Keith was Jamaican and they were too. So sending me down to cop wasn't a thing to them.

I used to always smell the outside of the package, I liked the smell. I watched Keith roll up spliffs, sometimes in a trance but most of the time he would smoke it in the pipe. He had a nice one too, a little marble joint. He always had a little residue left inside the pipe. I would pick it up and pretend to smoke from it. My moms didn't know this though, I was sneaky.

I felt slick this particular day so I grabbed a 10 cent coin and went to see the Rastas. I knocked on the door and told them Keith wanted a dime. They started cracking up, invited me in, and offered me a tote on this big spliff that looked like a baseball bat.

I grabbed it, inhaled, and started choking up a storm. Basically, I fumbled, but automatically I asked for a rematch. And, they were impressed. So much so that I was shown another room of the house, the kitchen. Big triple beam scales, pounds of weed and cocaine was on the table being bagged up.

Dread offered me a QP, and told me to bring him back $200. I didn't know much about hustling at that point, but I caught on quickly. Just by eye measuring the product, I knew it was a good idea. He even gave me a hundred packs of manila envelope bags to make dime bags. He said the next ones will cost me $20. Which seems very fair considering I will be making money.

Next time Keith gave me $10 to cop a dime from downstairs I would fake like I was actually going and serve him from my pack. I couldn't wait to go to school the next day.

I stayed for an hour then asked to go to the bathroom, I was out. I went to the projects, that was my new class. It was like a world within the world. Two chicks were banging out, titties popped out of 1 girl shirt. She kept going like she didn't even care. The crowd was huge, and nobody was trying to stop them.

Afterwards, it was business as usual, cars were pulling up, people were walking up, everybody serving what they had for sale. I saw some dude with money, I don't know what they had, but it was booming.

I was lucky like you wouldn't believe. It appears, the dude that sold weed ran out. Now all his customers are roaming around like zombies, which was a heck of a lot of people. I heard this dude say "damn nobody got weed out here?" I went for it, "yo I've got it", the crowd just formed around me. I probably should have been scared but I wasn't. I got excited. So many people were handing me $10 bills, it was crazy.

Some wanted 10 bags and some wanted 5 at a time and 2 hours later I sold out. I didn't even count my money, but I knew it was there and that was good enough for me.

Two cats from Nelton Court approached me asking who I was, and where I was from, I told them. I guess me being a little dude saved me from getting robbed. Also, they were impressed with my heart. Nobody just opens up shop without permission in someone else's hood, nobody.

They asked me if I could get more weed, which I could easily. My connect was stacked up with pounds! I didn't tell him that though. The next day I left school again with the same routine for maybe a week. I was making dreads $200 and $300 for me, it was crazy. I sold out every day before school let out. Only thing I liked about going to school was bringing big bags of candy and giving it away mostly to the girls, and making my escape!

Dread couldn't believe I was moving the way I was, but I was. By now I'm getting 3 pounds and paying only $700 a pound. A $100 discount for my efforts.

This one sunny afternoon, the projects got raided, everybody scattered. I didn't know where to go, but these older dudes who knew I had the weed told me to follow them. Their crib was the spot, everybody went there to smoke and play video games and Gamble.

I went from one gate to another gate, everybody smoked and these were the ones making the money. So I struck oil all over again. They were gambling on Pac-Man, $100 a game. I just watched at first thinking they were crazy for betting their money so easily. But then, I saw an opportunity. This one guy that I guess was the champion was taking all challenges. Or all suckers' bets. He never lost. But I played much better than him, I used to play my brother Taki all night sometimes and kick his butt. So I let him beat me the first game, then asked if he wanted to bet $300 on the next one, he went for it. I smoked his ass! All of the cats were crowded around watching us play. It was live. Then I won. And everybody got quiet. "What!? The champ got beat?"

He was almost foaming at the mouth. At first I thought he wasn't going to pay me the way I beat him. But he paid. And on top of that, I sold all my smoke out. It was a good day

Every day now, I will stop at the spot and maintain my crown. The same dude I beat for his spot was still challenging me, but 4 coins now, no more of that $300 a pop. Now he wanted to play for $50, that was still good though free money is free money.

By now, I'm not only selling dimes I'm selling QP's, but for $300. I still needed my profits. The school started talking to my moms a lot, I've been absent now for like a month. My moms was threatening me, and said she was going to start bringing me to school and sit in the class with me if I didn't stop.

So I went for a month straight, it was driving me crazy being there. I couldn't stop thinking about money and what I was missing out on in the streets. I started a fight and got suspended for a week. yes! Back in the hood.

My mom told me I couldn't go outside and had to tape her soap operas with the VCR for her, but I still snuck out when she left. Remember the dude who was selling weed before my arrival? Well, he couldn't take it anymore. Everybody fell in love with my cute self, and on top of it all, I had better, greener smoke and my bags were unbeatable!

He played me. His name was Dirt so I should have known better than to trust him. He asked me to meet him in the abandoned building on this side street, next to the projects. I came like a fool with a QP.

He pulled out this rusty gun that probably didn't even work, but I wasn't going to find out the hard way. So I gave it up. He wanted my money also but I ran off, he wasn't getting both.

That shook me up a little. I fell back from the projects and started going to school a little just to get my moms off my case. Plus, I made a few dollars; after all I was only eleven years old. I had nice clothes, Shoot Dogs, Adidas, Pumas, Lee Jeans, Buds and Kangols. All that, plus my mom still kept me fresh.

One day, I faked like I fell down the stairs. I just didn't feel like going to school. My moms called the ambulance, and we ended up going to the Housing Authority. But after they settled with my mom's, we got evicted from the apartment building. We were moving to this project called Bellevue Square.   Hold   on!!

2 BELLEVUE SQUARE

I came with my moms to check out my new stomping grounds. It was wild. We lived in Building 21 apartment k on the fourth floor. The Mailroom was something else, kind of scary. Sort of like an open hallway with safety deposit boxes, minus the safety.

They had a few basketball courts. This guy named Johnny Dukes had this spot where you could get trained to box. He was a well-known figure in Hartford courts, as well as the underworld. Rumors were, his people were mobbed up, but that wasn't no rumor trust me.

As we were walking back to our soon to be new spot I was catching all types of stares and rolling eyes. My moms was trying to hold my hand, but I had to pull away as gently as possible. A week later we went there. All types of cats were trying to help us move our things out the truck. But I knew better. They were appraising us, figuring out how much our shit was worth.

A lot has happened in recent years, for instance, Keith Fly, my sisters Val and Nadia's pops was killed by a tractor trailer. He was a great dude. Actually, he was the best.

May god be pleased with Keith Fly. Amen!!

School was rather unique. First of all, it was like smurf huts or houses right there in the projects. Literally a hop skip and a jump. Even though I was young, the teenage dudes were not feeling me at all.

I stayed fresh and was very confident. The first day of school was weird. I'll never forget my teacher Mr. Brown, he was Irish and had a fluffy red beard. He was short but tough. I hated when he called me to the board to do math in front of the class. Even though I knew what I was doing, I was still nervous. Nyesha Smith was the flyest piece in the class, red thing.

I wasn't trying to get her attention, I had her attention, fully. Her and her girls in the class would stare at me any and everywhere I walked. The lunchroom, the classroom, gym, everywhere. I hated after school, all the dirty cats would get together and beat me down. Rip my clothes up, even pull my hair like a chick.

I used to get beat down! Coming in the house swollen and black and blue. This didn't happen to my brothers, just me. I was the different one. But I wasn't going to keep allowing this to occur.

I still had my weed stacked up from before, but I was mostly just smoking it now being that I didn't have any clientele at the moment. I needed some eazy-wider sheets to roll up, but I still couldn't go into the bodega and buy them myself.

There was this dude standing by the payphone watching every chick breeze by. Trying to give away his number, but nobody wanted it. Anyway, I asked him to buy the sheets for me and gave him the money.

When he gave them to me he asked, "who these for?" His name was Chuck, he was like 24. I told him I had weed and did he know a place we could smoke with some girls?

He happened to be from Bellevue Square also, the next building over actually, building 14k. He had four sisters and they all were way older than me, except one. I liked Trisha, she was light skinned with brown hair, maybe 14-15 years old, real cute. She had a little body too. She talked fast, so did I.

Soon as I came in, she sat right next to me, she really was hawking the spliff I was trying to light. I took a few massive totes and passed it to her. Her eyes got big when she tasted that greeny-green.

I let Chuck light up his own piece. I wanted to ping pong with his sister. Her red lips made the spliff kind of wet when she passed it back. I didn't mind though. For me, that was equivalent to a kiss.

We were all twisted in no time! Then like 3 more women came through the door. Another one of Chuck's sisters, his cousin E-Lon from Cali, and their friend Tori who was staying at Chuck's mom crib with her sons.

I love it, I'll let them all smoke. All eyes were on me when I pulled out my QP and kept rolling up. Chuck's next door neighbors were Jamaicans, this cat named "Kim", they sold smoke and had a booming ass gate. Chuck assumed that I got the smoke from him, but it was my own supply.

I didn't want the day to end, but I had to go home. I had school the next day which I dreaded. I was dragging my feet, not really in a rush to be there, when I saw a brown paper bag in the bushes like someone tried to stash it there. They clearly didn't do a good job.

I grabbed it, it was a .38 snub nose, yes, even though thus far I never dealt with a gun, I was a proud new owner of a black revolver. It only had 3 bullets, but that would do just fine. Talk about a pep in my step. I was gliding! Trust me.

"Steven Keaton" was one of the main bullies on my case. Him and his friend "Chelo". This dude was a few years older than us, but was a giant! They just knew it would be the same typical type of day. Talk shit to me, then beat me down when the bell rang. Not today! I couldn't wait for the bell to ring today!

Nyesha Smith was close by and Steven Keaton was trying to show off for her, talking slick, that's when my bravery levels went way up to the roof. I punched him in the face as hard as I could. It felt great! Guess what? Steven Keaton cried like a chick, wow!

He yelled out, "after school me and Chelo gonna kill you". I just laughed at him, you should have seen this look of shock on his face. He was steamed-up. I was ready.

Finally the bell rang. Kids in my time couldn't resist seeing someone get beat down in front of everybody, as long as it wasn't them. Well, today would be interesting.

The crowd trapped me in like always, but this time I wasn't scared at all. I was smiling at them. Nobody understood why until they got close up on me and I pulled out. They must've thought the gun was fake until I aimed, pointed it straight at Chelo's head and squeezed. But damn, I missed. I really was mad! The crowd scattered, including them suckers. I was the only one standing.

I went to Chuck's later, smoked the house out and bragged about my day so far. Chuck didn't believe me until I flashed the steel on him. He was scared as fuck. Trisha looked like she was turned on. I was. She wanted to hold it, but I couldn't do that. Even Chuck asked, but I wasn't about to give up my power. Not even for a brief moment.

I still had a few dollars, but I wanted to hustle. Chuck's cousin E-Lon was bad, she looked Puerto Rican, but was black. Sexy. She played me but I didn't care, she used to kiss me and say I was her man. I believed her too! Buying her pizza when she was hungry. Sneakers, mostly reeboks back then and giving her like 60 beans for the pocket made me feel huge. And no one else had it for her, not even the older cats I saw her creeping off with.

I was coming to check her, and found her in the hallway kissing up on this punk named "Peter Wheat", an older cat. She started laughing when I caught them kissing, he did too. Until I pulled out, aimed at his head and popped his hat right off his head. No lie. He hauled ass. Left her standing there, but she didn't have anything to worry about. I never laid a hand on a girl, ever! And wouldn't.

I had to start forgetting about E-Lon, she was dangerously beautiful. Trisha heard what happened and now she felt a little jealous. She started playing me next, but that only went on for so long before I pulled the plug.

Chuck knew I had heart and wanted to get some money with me so he vowed, "soon we would start being stick up kids". As long as we ate, I didn't care. I was running out of weed and money. Something had to give.

I only had one bullet left, Chuck paid someone to get us a box, but I still wouldn't let him hold it down. Not yet anyway.

Today I wasn't going to school, my .38 was full, and my pockets were empty. But not for long.

We waited in Chuck's hallway, it was the third of the month, and Friday. Two white dudes went to cop weed from Kim. As they were coming down the stairs, we ran up on them. No masks.

"Let me get that weed you just copped plus your bread." From the looks in their eyes, they wanted to take off. "Try to make it out the hallway". But I was itchy, I saw the one closest to me, and squeezed at his leg. Instantly he screamed and gave up what I requested. Which was $700 and an ounce of smoke. The other dude chanted something religious I think and gave me what he had, which was $500 and a bunch of bagged up dime bags of weed. I took it all.

We ran to Chuck's house, which was only upstairs. The dudes hauled ass out the hallway and took off in their car frantically. I kind of felt bad, but my excitement outweighed my guilt. The way Chuck kept avoiding eye-contact. I could tell he was shook, but I couldn't turn on him.

I told Chuck we should go downtown and buy some clothes, he was down, so we left. On the way, we passed by a check cashing place. Chuck had an idea, there was this old man, Chuck suggested we follow him, we did but I wasn't comfortable with it.

Finally, we were in this like, wooded path closed off by a parking lot. Chuck sucker punched the man, but the man fought back hard, he wasn't giving his wallet-up, so Chuck and the old man were tussling. He gave chuck a good run for his money, what I mean is the man was a fighter. Chuck looked at me for a second like, he needed my help with the man but I couldn't at all. I wasn't crossing that line.

Chuck knocked him out and got the wallet, it had 1500 dollars in it. Chuck knew about social security checks, I didn't, and I didn't want to know either. This was low.

I felt weird even being present, we skipped the shopping spree and headed to Chuck's again. We were jogging, adrenaline on 1000. This older guy was jogging, also towards us, and for no reason at all, Chuck clotheslined this guy. The man falls straight to the back of his head, smacks the curb and dies.

But what was even crazier is, we were right in front of the graveyard, and across the street from our project.

The man's body was there even after they chalked up the scene and the Crime Scene Investigators came, then eventually the coroner. At least 8 hours had passed before that sidewalk had become a regular sidewalk again. I felt bad. I cursed Chuck out for hours. I told him, I don't respect his work and the targets he chose.

Weed was definitely my medicine, I was getting out of control fast, and it was only the beginning. My mother knew nothing, my whole family knew nothing, only Chuck.

It's about to get crazy, hold on. You have NO Idea!

3 NEW HAVEN

The Channel 3 news crew came through the projects asking questions about the guy who got killed the other day. News travels fast, especially bad news. Little kids in the hood excited to be speaking on camera were shooting off words like an oozie, saying "Chucky and the new kid did it, they over there".

I needed out of that crowd fast. My cousin Paige came to visit the family from New Haven. She was older, my mother's age actually. It was my first time meeting her. I knew I had family in New Haven, but hadn't met them all yet. Cousin Paige had 3 kids back at home. 2 daughters in their early 20's and a son a little younger than me.

I fell back from the crime spree for a second. With the money me and Chuck robbed for, we bought coke to hustle. Chuck knew a guy and we copped a few ounces at a fairly reasonable price I guess. We bagged up big 20's. As it stood, we could've both made a few thousands each.

We started slanging in Chucks hallway, right in front of Kim's door. It was surely disrespectful, but I didn't care at that point. Kim mostly sold bagged up stuff, dimes, half ounces, ounces, etc. But mostly gave deals with the dimes. I noticed people were asking for powder sometimes and that's where I stepped in.

Few sales here and there, a few hundreds, then, they started coming often. What I'm thinking is, since I was young, I gave them more coke than what they were accustomed to for the price they were spending. And, I didn't know about stretching coke to make more profits, so me not cutting it was extra beneficial, on all levels.

I would sneak out at night to catch sales in the hallway. Had my bodyguard with me, my trusty .38 snub nose, and my medicine, greeny green.

I met this lady named Lucy. An Older Spanish woman, she got crazy high, coke and dope. And she drank alcohol, but she would run me sales, customers. Basically, people she knew who were not the cops and almost all of them got high with her. So basically, win win for all parties concerned.

Lucy was married to an old Spanish man. All he did was work hard and come home and drink himself to sleep. He didn't get high at all, opposites really do attract, I see. Anyway, Lucy had 3 sons. One of them, the oldest, Angel, was the same age as me. He knew what his moms was into, and even that she worked for me, but somehow it didn't bother him at all.

His step pops had a nice station wagon, up to date joint. Angel would take the keys at night and me, him and this kid Ricky who lived in my building would ride around smoking weed acting grown. It was fun, we did this almost everyday. Angel drove very well to be 11 going on 12.

I just knew I could drive too, I hadn't tried yet, but I had plans. This one night, we didn't drive, we just walked around the projects and smoked, hung out in the hallway while I caught sales. Chuck popped up, he hung out with us although it seemed odd, being he was way older.

Ricky's mom and sisters were calling out to him to get in the house, but he hid amongst us staying out. About an hour later, you wouldn't believe what happened.

Usually I didn't allow anyone to lay hands on my gun. But I let Angel hold it. Big mistake. He pointed it at me. I barked on him, he then pointed it at Chuck. Chuck yelled at him as well, then he pointed it at Ricky. Ricky got scared and ran, that's when Angel popped off 2 shots in Ricky's direction. At first we thought they planned out a sick trick which wasn't funny at all. Ricky fell flat by the dumpsters. We thought he was playing around, but sadly, he wasn't. He was hit in the back. I snatched the gun back from Angel and ran off. I was scared, everybody ran, leaving Ricky on the ground.

People in the projects were all looking out the windows and seen enough to call the ambulance and the police. I'm not going to lie, I was scared. I ran to my cousin's house on the Avenue. I told him what happened, stayed over, and went home the next day.

Since Ricky stayed on the 3rd floor, and me on the 4th, I stopped by his moms to check on his recovery status. But when that door came open, actions spoke louder than words. His sisters and mom were all crying hysterically.

But yet I asked anyway, "Is Ricky alright?" His sister Sandra yelled at me, "Ricky died", I couldn't believe what I was just told. I was numb for sure. Started crying right then and there, saying, "I'm sorry".

His sisters said, "you killed my brother!" I ran upstairs, told my moms what happened, but she already knew and had something to say. Also, the homicide detectives came by looking for me and they were coming back until they found me. It seems people spread the rumor that me and Chuck did it. So now, everybody who didn't like me before, really hated me now. And, it seemed, with good reason. Everybody knew I had the gun. I hid it, and called the homicide on myself to answer any questions they might have, or had.

Angel already turned himself in and told them he shot Ricky by mistake though. The detectives knew what happened already but they wanted to know where the gun was. I played stupid but felt so sad that Ricky actually died behind my gun.

I went to his funeral. His whole family, even those that flew in from Puerto Rico were giving me death stares. Everybody still thought I did it. All they knew was that the gun was mine, and they were right.

All this occurred while my cousin Paige was in town visiting. What a first impression, right? She offered to let me come cool off in her house for a few months in New Haven. At that time, I rejected the offer, but it floated around in my mind for days to come.

Me and Chuck was walking down Main St. when this fool pulled up to the curve talking crazy. He asked me and Chuck if we could loan him some money for his father's operation. A total stranger, talking to us as if we were his near relatives. Chuck suggested we get in the car. And like a fool, I did. I had a bright idea, go to the spot where I buried my gun, take this car and go live in New Haven with cousin Paige. And that's what we did, we jacked him for the car. Hopped on the highway and headed straight to New Haven.

Mid-way, Chuck pulled over on the shoulder of the road and asked if I could drive? I said yes, and so was put to the test. We switched spots and I started driving. I was nervous, but I did watch people while they drove so I was good.

Off to New Haven. When we got to the exit, I admit I wasn't as prepared as I thought. I turned too wide and smacked just a little into these sand barrels. But not enough to destroy the car. I didn't even dent it up, just some scratches.

It was a 1984 Chevy Spectrum, it was nice, free of charge, and at the time, mine.

It took about a half hour, but I found my cousin Paige's spot. She lived on Howard Ave, right across the street from the fire station. Her daughters were pretty, my cousins Linda and Lori. Lori had a daughter, Shenice. Linda didn't have any children.

I introduced Chuck. It kind of looked like I had a bodyguard. I knew Paige smoked because I smelled it in the house as soon as I walked in. I asked permission first, but once she said it was alright, I sparked up the whole house. I could tell my cousin's liked me. They kept staring at me, and Chuck kept staring at them.

They invited some of their friends over. They were all older than me, in their early 20's. I was only 11 ½ soon to be 12 going on 30.

Lori's friends were saying repeatedly they wish I was older. I knew what that meant and wouldn't forget it when I was actually older. Since we carjacked that dude for the automobile, we had the keys so we appeared legit, even though we were far from that.

12

Lori's girlfriends stayed overnight. The next day they were waiting for cabs to come take them home. I told them there was no need. I had a car. They busted out laughing, but when I told them to look out the window it wasn't that funny of a joke.

So we dropped them off. I got better at driving just that fast. I didn't want to look foolish in front of those cuties.

On the way back to Howard Ave, it was drizzling and we saw two women, daughter and mother. They were struggling with groceries. Even though we did a lot of dirt, we both had soft spots for women in distress. I pulled over and asked the ladies if we could help them. They let us drive them home. They were bad, the daughter's name was Connie. I forgot the moms name, but Chuck got the moms and I had the daughter.

We brought the groceries inside their apartment. It was small, but nice and clean. The lady had twin boys and her daughter Connie. Oh yeah, Connie had a 3 year old baby. Connie was 17 at the time. They were from North Carolina and I loved their accent.

We left to buy more weed, they already had drinks. Plus, they cooked for us that night. The food was delicious, and I was impressed. Then the twins went to bed, and Chuck slid off with the moms while Connie invited me to watch a movie in the living room with her.

It was a porno. I snuck and watched my moms pornos, but never watched with a young lady before. I was very excited to say the least. My eyes were glued to the screen when Connie lifted the covers and disappeared.

Introducing me to oral sex. I'm hooked for life. Then she introduced me to regular sex, also hooked for life. She was well experienced, and a great teacher. Connie was something else.

The next day, Chuck told me he knew some girls in New Haven and wanted to go check them. Now Chuck liked big women, real, real big women. To each his own, but I wasn't around for that. I thought it wouldn't be fair to only see the people I wanted and not see his people, so we planned to go pick his people up later.

Meanwhile, we went to this bodega on Liberty street, next to the jungle. This white dude seemed very much out of element, he had on a green suit, he was very tall. I could see the print of his wallet. We followed him to this abandoned school pathway. Sort of a short cut. I told him, "run your wallet". He made a racist comment, maybe he did, or maybe I wanted to think he did, anyway.

I aimed at his chest, and his head got hit. He fell. I didn't even grab the wallet, I ran off and dropped the gun right there. Me and Chuck took off, hopped in the car and went to go check the girls he knew.

Before we got there, I asked Chuck, "are they huge?" He laughed and lied, "nah, they're straight". Soon as we pulled up, two big mamas were sitting on this porch looking hungry. Starving for attention.

Chuck introduced me, I was pissed, but mostly thinking of Ricky and what I had just done. So not paying attention while driving, I ran a stop sign and t-boned this Lincoln Continental. We fled and left the big girls stuck in the Spectrum. I ran straight to my cousin Paige's house. Chuck went his own way. One of the big girls already knew Chuck's full name. Basically, he's hit. They didn't know me. I was hiding in the attic smoking my last weed up. When my cousin Lori said, "the cops were downstairs asking for me". I didn't want to get my people in trouble, so I came down to face the music.

They took me straight to the precinct on Whalley Ave, I got fingerprinted, and thrown in a holding cell. They gave me one call. It was standard procedure. I called my moms, apologizing for being a terrible kid. She cried, so did I.

The cops just assumed I was 16 because of my height, and I didn't tell them otherwise, just went with the flow of things.

4 LONG LANE

After being in a freezing cold cell for maybe 8 hours, two detectives came to see me. They were puzzled, my prints were just matched in their database with the prints off of the .38 found on the scene of a crime on Liberty St. which of course, I forgot all about.

This was the avalanche of my problems. The car accident, carjacking, assault, and a few other things weren't in comparison with the charges I faced concerning the shooting. What stumbled the detectives was the fact that I was a Juvenile, and really, being booked and fingerprinted as an adult was a huge mistake on their part.

I was immediately taken out of the holding cell on Whalley and brought to the Juvenile facility across the street. I really didn't understand their foul-up at that time. I was young, dumb, and had a lot on my mind. Can you imagine?

My court date was scheduled for the next business day. It was a Friday, so that meant I was in store for a very different type of weekend.

I had to share a cell with this kid from New Haven, he was maybe 15 years old, but a big kid. He talked a lot, bragged about how he stabbed his mom's boyfriend for beating up his moms. Normally, I would've felt some compassion for his compassion, but he thought he could bully me first. Then tried to outsmart me on getting my breakfast in the morning.

Which was Saturday morning special. I found out the hard way, donuts and cereal. We only got donuts once a week, so when it came around, all the so called tough guys would either take or manipulate their way into everyone else's. I wasn't having it.

My celly had already told his buddies from his hood that I was from Hartford and there was already an established feud between Hartford and New Haven youth. Apparently, from the youths to the adults in prison. So while I stayed back in the cell a little longer than my celly so I could brush my grill, he sped out to set me up with his crew.

15

Four people could sit at a table, so usually people who knew each other would sit together. I understood the logic of that. However, down there the whole block of youths was from New Haven and I was the only outsider, minus a few white boys who really didn't count because they were easy victims.

They would make reservations the night before to just give their food up and drink coffee.

So each time a seat was available, I was asking out of respect, "is someone sitting here already?" and each time, someone would say "you can't sit there", I would swallow my pride and move on to the next table. Humbly.

But fuck that, I couldn't take it anymore! I sat wherever I wanted. The first person that came up telling me to move I punched in the face. Now I'm getting it on.

After I set it off, the first kid fell back holding his face. A little blood was on his shirt. That only fueled his mans and them. The next kid hit me in the face, I tackled him down. I had the better position, so basically, this kid was lunch meat for me. I blacked out, not realizing I was banging the kids head on the floor. I just wouldn't stop doing it, until the staff, after observing for maybe 10 minutes finally tackled me off of him and restrained me.

Damage was done. I didn't have to look at the other kid, I could see the expression on the other kids on the block faces. They were trembling and staring at me.

I didn't want this, but I had to defend myself. These dudes preyed on the weak, and that wasn't me at all. Since I had blood all over me from the fight, they made me take a shower and gave me different clothes to put on. I felt better, more leveled.

I wanted to go back to the cell I was in before, but when they asked the kid inside already, he refused. All that big mouth for nothing. Now he was scared. So they put me in the cell by myself.

It was cool I guess. Every time I came to the door, which had a little view of the block and the rest of the cell's doors, I noticed people at their windows staring at me.

It was almost lunch time, cheeseburgers and tater tots. I was hungry. Once they popped my cell open, I ran up on my old celly. Caught him slipping. He still had his food tray in hand. I clocked him in the mouth, more blood, I didn't stop until they peeled me off of him.

They locked down the block again. Made everybody eat in their cells. Took me back to the showers, I felt like the cleanest kid on the block. They gave me another set of clothes.

This time, they came at me with pepper spray in hand, and cuffs, and said, "next time you do this, we are beating your ass ourselves. So think about that one." I did. These were some big dudes! They all looked like they had just got out of jail themselves.

16

Back to my single cell. Time flew. Dinner time. The shift had changed, so the staff was different. They immediately came to my cell deep and asked, "are we gonna have any more problems with you?" I said no.

They let me out for dinner and I had a table all to myself. And since the block was so small, the kids I fought were still there and had to see my face. I didn't mind, but I could tell they were shook so I stayed on point. Usually you had the option to wear shower clogs they gave you, or your sneakers. But they took everyone's sneakers and made us wear the clogs or our socks. I came out barefoot, for the grip, just in case they tried to jump me.

After a few court trips, and crazy more stress, I took the plea deal which considering the severity of my situation wasn't bad at all. I would stay in the custody of the state until I could no longer, which was, till I was 16 years old. Then my time would be up.

A lot happened in the year 1984, it was December, I finally turned 12 a.k.a 21. And the next week I would be in this reform school called Long Lane in Middletown, Connecticut.

All the kids were scared to go there. They called it Gladiator's school, so I would find out very soon if its reputation was warranted or not.

The day I was transferred was freezing. I was in the back seat with a cage dividing me and the social worker and the doors were definitely locked. I wasn't surprised. Had they not been, I would've been out.

Long Lane's compound resembled a college campus. I saw kids coming back from the mess hall which is called the Chow Hall, it's where we eat. They were all lined up as if they had been in the military. The cottages reminded me of how the schools were set up in my project, like smurf huts or houses.

After the social worker handled some paperwork in the front offices, Long Lane's staff, which were a security team called APO's. It stood for Agency Police Officers and I would learn later on in my stay there, that they had no problem beating you down. Trust me!

They escorted me to my cottage. All the cottages had different names. Mine was called "Smith", and since they placed me on the B-side, I was in Smith-B. It was the twilight zone. I was labeled an SJO which meant Serious Juvenile Offender. So they wouldn't hesitate to beat me up.

They would bring me to a more locked down part of the compound called the unit. The unit had 3 parts to it 1, 2, and 3. It was said that the unit was no joke. If you fought there, they wouldn't break it up until both of you are finished.

As soon as I came into Smith cottage the staff did intake. Afterwards the whole block was ordered to sit in a circle and introduce itself. The group was very diverse, but mostly dudes from the hood, town to town.

They also had this brainwashing system they called GGI (Guidance Group Intellect. They held GGI daily. And other prisoners could call a group on you where you would have to circle up and give a person feedback on how to rectify their behavior.

Then the person would come up with an action plan on how they would specifically correct themselves and the group would have to take consensus and the majority would have to agree that the person's action plan would suffice. But if the group didn't agree on it, the person would have to take advisory to an action plan or come up with another one until everybody agreed.

It was very different and would take some getting used to.

We had single rooms, very tight, and we wore our own street clothes. I needed some brought to me. People that earned it, could go on passes for hours with a sponsor or earn a weekend pass home. But, usually a good portion of your commitment had to be served before being eligible for this.

I had a journey before me. I couldn't even consider the thought, but I was annoyed seeing other people leave on passes and come back with new clothes. You also could get sneakers and boots. I needed some clothes.

Dude was trying to be funny and called a group on me. So we had to circle up. I was pissed. Dude started laughing at me. I grabbed my wooden chair and broke it on his face and shoulders. The group was stunned, maybe that was a first to them.

The kid fell out. But he was alright. Mostly his ego was bruised, his face a little.

APO's came into the cottage, rushed me, beat me down, and brought me to isolation. Oh yeah, isolation smelled like horse shit. I was stripped naked. I wanted   to   die.

5 STILL IN LONG LANE

In some aspects Long Lane babied you. In most cases, you were treated like an animal. Isolation always brings the worst out of you. People even look at you differently. If you got what's called a "Major", you were brought to the unit for a stay.

A major was achieved when you went to isolation four or five times in a certain period of time. I had that, and now a trip to the unit was sanctioned. They gave me 90 days in the unit, it was wild.

Crazily the unit had a pool table. You still had to do GGI, but the blocks were way smaller than the cottages. A lot less people to deal with. Single cell status.

They made us go to school, and the extra good news about that was the fact that it was coed. Well not exactly, but close enough. The girls were right across the hall from us and you could sneak and speak to them briefly. Even write from cottage to cottage with them.

The name of their cottage was Craig. If you maintained a clean setting and behaved, once a month the girls could come over and be in the basement with us. In the basement we had a pool table, a radio, ping pong table etc., wasn't bad.

I was writing to a few girls. There was only one female cottage and like 6 male cottages. Oftentimes the same girl would be writing 10 dudes or more depending on how cute she was. This led to a lot of fights.

People even escaped from the place from time to time. Sometimes attempts were made, but some got caught in the process. Almost making it home.

Usually if you act up, fight, or curse out the staff etc., you would go to isolation. Isolation was the dungeon. Straight up. Tight, constricted space with a metal bed frame in the middle of the room. No mattress, and freezing cold, always.

Often you would get stripped down naked, full points restrained. This was torture. I know.

I had a fight or two, but overall, the 90 days went by fast. Now I'm going back to the hill. Back to Smith-B.

Some of the people who were there before had left. And of course, their beds filled up fast. New batch of prisoners.

I was only a year in, but I was thinking about escaping. A few cats I was alright with had taken off and made it and I figured, if they could make it, so could I. I needed new clothes, money, and definitely weed.

I called my moms every now and then but it hurt to hang up the phone, so I avoided it as much as I could. My brothers and sisters barely knew me and I felt alone in this world. Though all the bad choices were mine, and I owned them.

My mindset was, I'm out. After dinner, we were about to go back into the cottage, and I took off. Jumped the hedges, there were no barb wires on the hill, only in the unit. Only the unit was considered high security. A few dudes took off when I did, didn't expect that. The staff automatically grabs the radio, walkie talkie, and calls the APO's. Then they go on a manhunt in the town of Middletown to return you.

The APO's were nearby and they had the dogs for assistance. They were on us. I was up in a tree while these other two dudes got caught, I could see them from where I was hiding.

The dogs were barking like crazy, but they didn't look up so no one saw me. But I watched as this one dude called the APO and looked straight at me. I know he told on me. They came straight to the tree. Come on buddy, come down. At this point it wouldn't have made any sense to stay up in the tree, so I came down. Got cuffed and thrown into the APO's car. Back to the lane, Mission incomplete. I failed.

At first, they brought me to isolation, escape was an automatic major. Guaranteed trip to the unit, and the compound was a soap opera. Everybody knows your business, so by the morning, the girls would know what time it was.

I stayed in the unit for a year this time. I could have gotten out in 6 months, but I kept getting into trouble. Mostly fights. We all had a lot of energy. It's expected.

Believe it or not, the year flew by. Before you know it, I was back on the hill. At this time, the cottage had flipped, meaning a lot more people went home since my arrival. Now I had to get re-established in Smith-B.

It was 1986 and hip hop was getting bigger than ever! We had social room time on the weekends where we could watch TV in the morning, after breakfast. The social room was really the living room.

We used to watch "YO MTV Raps with Fab-5 Freddy" on Saturday's. All the rap videos. This was the highlight of the weekend besides watching movies in the social room at night before bed.

I'll never forget these two female staff we had, one was Ms. Driscoll. She had a big gap between her teeth, nice, old school down south, black woman. She spoke with an accent and was as sweet as can be. She always tried to talk me out of getting into trouble. And no matter what, she didn't give up on me. She actually calmed me down on a few occasions where I could have really self-destructed. Thank you Ms. Driscoll, wherever you are on earth.

The other was Mrs. Bess, she was surely old school. Put you in the mind frame of your grandmother. She talked pure shit to you, and pissed you off when she made you clean something to her standards. Which were very high, might I add. But in the long run, you would realize she was right on point and she only tried to help you, sincerely. She was no joke. She would make you cry if you were weak. Thank you Mrs. Bess wherever you are on this earth.

I couldn't stand wearing the same clothes everyday anymore all year round. So I had to escape. It was a fashion emergency.

Now it was '87, time was flying. Since I stayed out of stuff for a while, I got upgraded to a so-called, "better room". Where 4 prisoners lived instead of just an individual. It had an easier escape side of things. For instance, we had a fake balcony. "Why they do that?"

A week after being in that new room I jetted. Me and this kid Peter from Norwalk escaped. I knew Peter liked to steal cars, and that was perfect.

We had a jump start because we left in the middle of the night so we probably didn't get reported to the APO's until the morning. Great leverage.

Peter knew where this Toyota dealership was that kept the keys to a few cars in the ignition. We got this burgundy Toyota Camry. '87, Brand new model. The dash was all lit up blue, it was nice. So first, Peter went to this apartment complex and siphoned some gas out of other car's tank. That was a first for me.

Then we went to his hometown. My first time out there. He changed clothes real quick, then we went to Bridgeport to this house party his friends were having. I wasn't into that, but I rolled with it. Next stop, Hartford, CT. "Home sweet home," seemed like I was gone for so long. The air was even different.

The projects looked crazy. Like a prison at night. I walked into my mom's apartment and everybody started crying. My sisters and brothers, my moms. They thought I got out the right way. But I told them I escaped and had to go back soon. I would get what I needed and turn myself in, which I did.

This dude named "Chill WIll" used to live in my building. He was a famous drunk in my head. He was also known for ranking on people and he could play basketball really good. He could dunk and all that, even though he wasn't tall. Chill Will didn't like me at all when I first moved there.

As time passed, I guess he realized I was alright after all he introduced me to "Country Kev". Country Kev sold dope. Not a lot of people liked him because he came from somewhere else and just got money. And like me, he wasn't asking for permission.

Country Kev got ear of my situation and capitalized. Gave me $3000 worth of dope and wanted me to bring him back $2000. Right in front of my building was the dope spot. So all I did was go in the hallway, serve the customer, and watch out for the cops.

I didn't have to go to school, so basically, I had the morning shift to myself. And for dope dealers, those early hours were important for business.

I ran around like a mad man. Hallway to hallway, stuffing my pockets as fast as I could. As soon as I made Kev's money I called, well beeped him for more.

He was loving my ambition. In 2 weeks, I had $5000 that was mine. And I ate good every day. I bought some clothes, boots, jackets, a few Kangol's, smoked weed every day and prepared myself to go back. I couldn't believe how big my sister and brothers had gotten. My moms was still looking young, and everybody still loved me.

Me and my cousin "Dogg" was coming from downtown. We saw these 2 girls. One was dark skinned and the other light skinned, Dogg knew them both, he introduced me. The dark skinned girl was Stacy; the other Dawn. I liked Dawn. Dawn didn't know it yet, but she would be my baby mother one day. Oh, and I told her that.

She was acting stuck up. Didn't want to talk, give me her number, nothing. But I wouldn't leave until she did. Finally, she forged a smile and hit me.

I must have talked to her on the phone for 8 hours a day. At least for 2 weeks straight. She invited me over for dinner. Her moms wanted to see who I was. We talked a little. I answered her questions. I think she liked me. She kept letting me come over every day. Her cooking was GREAT. And not long afterwards, I met the whole family.

I was like 2 years older than Dawn, so sex wasn't even a discussion. I was just happy to know her. You could tell she was going to be a great woman. I knew from day one.

She had a sister named Mara, a few years younger than Dawn. She was good people too, but we didn't talk much. I knew her uncle, Aunts, Grandmothers, all that.

Finally, I told her about Long Lane and I had to go back soon. Real soon, before I got in real trouble. She was sad, but said she would wait for me, write to me, and let me call her. I believed her.

All we did was kiss and talk on the phone a lot. I mostly told her about the future, how she would have a daughter with me. And love me forever.

Well, the day came. I copped some weed and some Army fatigues for the occasion. I had my clothes in a duffle bag and plastic bags. Sneakers in the boxes and underclothes, cosmetics. I called up Long Lane, and they came and got me.

It felt crazy being back in Long Lane. Since I turned myself in, they didn't take me to the unit. But I had to stay in the cottage for a week straight in the cell. No chow hall. Only School.

I couldn't wait to show off my new clothes and get my phone call privileges back. I wanted to tell Dawn what was up with me.

I not only had the weed, but I also had some paper on deck to roll up a spliff. Plus some matches and a lighter. Soon as I sparked up, the whole block smelled it, blowing me up, knocking on my cell door asking if I had more.

I was twisted, laughing and thinking about Dawn, how I got blessed on this round. I missed talking to her. I felt a little better about life. But I was still in the dark. Ms. Driscoll was still on my side; even after I escaped on her watch.

Mrs. Bess wasn't going to let me off that easily. She cursed me out, told me I didn't have any sense. She even smacked me upside my head. All I could do was laugh.

6 1989

My commitment is up. One last week in this miserable hole. I'm 16 now, no more of this kid shit from this point on. The judge would really drop that hammer on me.

I had no education at all. No real skills besides surviving in the streets and that ain't flying on applications. My moms picked me up. She took me to get pizza in Middletown before we headed home. It was good too!

I couldn't believe I was out. I didn't tell dawn or anything. I wanted to surprise her. That walk to her house felt like I was floating. Her moms answered the door, jaw dropped. She knew I was away, but no one expected me. Dawn wasn't home from school yet.

Ms. Cooper let me hide in her room. Her and her sister walked through the door, went to the fridge, talked junk to each other before they went into their rooms. Dawn walked in. I was behind the door. She slammed the door closed, I was standing there smirking.

She screamed a little, then rushed me. She was cute as fuck! Light skin, chinky eyes, thick thighs. She had on pink, white, and yellow. Flowery type tights.

We started kissing. I was super excited. You know what I mean, I had to sit down for a few.

Her sister came in, gave me a hug, but you could tell she was hating. Just a little. Ms. Cooper asked if I was staying for dinner. Dawn answered for me, she said "yes", I smiled.

Told me I couldn't leave. I was cool with that. Her moms boyfriend Tony was from my project. I know his nieces and stuff. He used to sit around, play video games and smoke weed. Dawn was showing off, helping her mother cook. It was real cute.

Tony invited me to play video games with him. I wasn't into video games like that, but he passed me the joint, I was definitely into that. I was twisted.

24

Ms. Cooper was cool as fuck. She didn't say anything about me smoking. Dawn kept going back and forth from the kitchen, to her moms room where we were blazing up. I caught her staring at me. I liked it.

They say "time flies when you're having fun" and it does. I had to go home. Ms. Cooper didn't tell me so, but I didn't want to be disrespectful.

Those kisses were like the greatest thing in the world to me. And I hated to stop. But I would be back, first chance I could. And I was.

Believe it or not, I kind of tried to do at least one or two human being things in my life. I enrolled myself in this school called "Delta". It was for knuckle heads such as myself.

I already knew, regular schools wouldn't accept me. First of all, I had less than a Junior high school education. I was troubled. And let's face it, a lot to deal with. I knew that and I understood their position.

I actually put in effort to be a regular attending student. My teachers weren't so friendly, but that wasn't what school was about. I came to learn something.

Old habits kicked in fast. I had no cash left and since I knew how to sell drugs, that door was always open if I chose to walk in.

Remember the drunk Chill Will? Well, last time he introduced me to Country Kev and I made a few dollars in that relationship, but I didn't want to sell dope again. I only capitalized before so rapidly because I took advantage of the early shift. You know, the hours where regular people go to work and attend school. Since I was giving school a shot, I didn't want to mess that up. Plus Dawn was proud of me for trying.

So Chill Will introduced me to Pook. Pook lived in building 28, a short cat, but had a big personality. First we started hanging out at his moms crib, smoking weed. Oh yea, his sister Tia was bad! Light skin cute thing, she had this laugh that would turn you on in a weird way. And she just knew she was bad.

Tia went to school with Dawn. They went to Hartford High. Sometimes Tia would come home from school and see us smoking in Pook's room. She always wanted to hit the weed and wouldn't slide until it was gone.

Pook sold weed, but just recently stepped up to selling coke. He let me make a few dollars here and there, but really wasn't in the position. I met Bilal, he lived on Main Street. He was older than me and had moved to CT from Texas. He was big out there, but I heard the laws were no joke.

Anyway, I started working for Bilal. He gave me a $1000 pack to try me out. Charged me $600. Basically, 60/40 split. Wasn't the worst pay, but my plans were bigger than staying content with that. I just needed some dollars to start my own thing.

Bilal's spot on Main Street was crazy. I could sell $10,000 worth of coke every day. Fast. Even on the weekends. I was moving up fast and smoking an ounce of weed a day. Serving coke up in the hallways, writing rhymes in between the time.

All that watching "YO MTV Raps" in Long Lane made me love hip hop. I could write pretty good, it was said. I used to battle dudes all the time in the Lane. Mostly showing off for the girls while destroying my competition. It was healthy.

Dawn used to like hearing me rhyme. Sometimes I would sit at her kitchen table and hit the beat at the same time. She even memorized my joints. That boosted my confidence.

Back in the projects, dudes started getting jealous again. My clothes were the best, I had the best coke, and on top of that I was getting a buzz on the street because of my music. I was going to the studio, making tapes every now and then.

Even Pook started coming to the studio and hopping on the mic. We started selling our tapes for 10 dollars. We couldn't Make enough. And some other drug dealers felt the music so much that they were willing to pay $40 for a tape.

The projects had this talent show every year on community day. It was a big event in the north end of Hartford. I killed it. Dawn was there, her moms, her mom's boyfriend Tony, Mara was there, Tia, Chill Will, Bilal, everybody in the hood was there. It was fun.

I got approached by this dude "Joe Young", he had this show called the "Joe Picture This Show". He got approached by Pepsi to come talk to me, but my head got big due to drug sales, and I ignored their offer. What a fool right? I know!

In the projects, sometimes the customers didn't have money to cop drugs, so they'd bring guns. Everybody wanted guns. I brought a few. This one night, a custy pulled up and tried selling me a .25 automatic, chrome joint.

Told me to get in the car. As we drove off, I asked what he wanted for the thing, but his price was ridiculous for such a small gun. I knew I would be getting it, one way or another.

I asked if I could hold it. This fool actually put that thing in my hand, and on top of that, it had shells. I cocked it back, squeezed at his leg. He screamed, and I jumped out.

Laughing on the way to Dawn's house, running fast as hell. That felt good, I know that wasn't nice.

I still hadn't had sex with Dawn yet and wasn't going to rush her. She was worth the wait. A few times, on the weekend, I was over so late that Ms. Cooper let me sleep on the couch.

Getting high on the way to school, I had to smell like a whole pound. They used to let us sit in the cafeteria before classes started. I was rapping, had the classmates vibing. When my teacher, Mr. Strong, this Polish bulldog looking dude started talking crazy to me.

I ignored him, kept entertaining the class. He came back with 4 other staff members. They started grabbing me and choking me then they slammed me hard on the floor. I couldn't believe what was happening. I kept saying "I can't breathe", they wouldn't stop choking me.

One of them had their knee in my spine. It was painful. They dragged me to this room. Full of matts on all the sides of the wall. They called it "time out". They took my boots and made me stand in the corner for 2 hours like I was a child. I was pissed off.

Every time I looked back at them to see their faces, they threatened me. "Turn back around or the time starts all over", they said. And they threatened to jump on me again if I didn't listen. I was tight.

I did it, just to get it over with. When the time was up, they gave me my boots and acted as if everything was normal. And they didn't just try to kill me. School had already let out.

I told them before I left the building, "I'm gonna kill y'all", and ran off. That whole day my balance was thrown off in the hallway. I didn't even watch out for the cops while I was serving. Even though it was booming, I didn't stay all day. I left with coke still in my possession, and I've never done that before. I just wanted to get away from things.

Went over to Pook's, smoked way too much. Then Tia came home early from school. As usual we got her sparked up. In her room she was playing this song me and Pook did. I made a mention of her in that particular song and it automatically became one of her favorites.

I went to Dawn's. Her aunt Brenda was there. I liked Brenda a lot. She was one of Dawn's youngest aunts and I smoked with her. And she always told her niece I was a keeper. She had good energy.

Her son Antwon looked just like me. I think that's the reason why Brenda liked me so much. Maybe I reminded her of her son's father. I heard he was "Big Time". Right now he's in the feds. Never met him before.

As usual, I smoked before school. I was twisted. I had a terrible feeling in my stomach about today. But life goes on.

Same two step, went to the cafeteria. Spit a few bars, blew a few minds and waited patiently for Mr. Strong to come pull that shit he pulled yesterday. I made eye contact. Screw it, my demon was out.

Everything went red for me. I pulled that little ass .25 Auto, pointed at Mr. Strong. He started pleading, "calm down, Mr. Ward", then he took off towards the classroom. Tried to plug him, bang, bang, bang, missed, damn. I just remember shells hitting the lockers.

The other staff ain't budge, Mouths open. Not a word. I looked their way. I wasn't even 2 feet away. Silence. The students were even silent. It was like I left my mind, then I returned.

"What the!" I ran out of the building, straight home. The next building over was the state troopers barracks. I glanced at the crown Victoria's as I sped by. Through downtown I ran past the YMCA all the way to the projects. Non-stop. I was numb.

7 IN THE SYSTEM

Here I go bringing problems to my doorstep again. My moms happens to be home today. I guess I was trying to explain what I did, but I always spoke fast and most people, including my moms couldn't understand what I was saying.

The phone rang, and from the way she was looking at me while listening to the other person on the other end. Someone must have been explaining what I did. Something told me to look out the window, the building was surrounded. Now should I fool myself, and pretend they weren't coming for me?

Nah, was all set, I knew it. They banged on the door so hard, you would have thought they paid rent. My moms was scared. I'm so bugged out, I told her don't worry and grabbed a steak knife.

She opened the door. They talked me into putting the knife down. I hated that I made my moms cry once again. I was crying too. They took me. As they were walking me downstairs cuffed up. I saw my brothers and one of my sisters. Now, they're crying.

My sister Val said, "let my brother go", It sounded so cute. And she was so serious. They brought me to the precinct, charged me with a bunch of shit. I was guilty of all of it.

They fingerprinted me, made me hold up that sign with the inmate number like in the movies. But this was real. I'll never forget this, the black cop lady at the window said, please empty your pockets young man.

Normally, a cop making a request such as empty your pocket isn't a dramatic scene, but in my case. Once I stuck my hands inside, I felt the $300 worth of coke I had left from the other day. Usually I didn't leave the spot until I was sold out.

But I was pissed that day from the school situation and just threw my routine way off. And now, my carelessness would cost me.

This was another charge itself. My bond was set and basically, I was set also. I discharged the firearm. Attempted first degree assault. Threatening. And now, possession of narcotics. It didn't matter what the bond was set at, I wasn't posting.

That night I went to Morgan St. This was a nasty rat infested, should be condemned Jailhouse. The blocks were real cell blocks with bars, and they were super tight.

Morgan St. is where they hold you until they send you to Hartford County Jail, The Metals. They had dorms and cell blocks. The dorms were for people who had small bonds. While the main building housed people with huge bonds. This is where I was headed.

The day I got moved to The Metals was a rainy day. I heard lots of stories, but I would now experience for myself, unfortunately. Since I was only 16 going on 17, I had to go to the youth tier.

There were 2 sides of the jail for the youth, East, or West. I was sent to West-2. They called it the wild wild west. Mostly kids from the north end were over there, and cats from the south end usually went to the east side.

Fights would pop off on both sides daily, but the real danger was in the west, clearly. Everybody knew that. They had single cells and 2 man cells. They put me in a cell with this Muslim dude from Bloomfield.

His name was Ahmad Compton, but we called him Shabazz. Cat was like 6' 5", but a real humble dude. He had a shooting too. But he actually hit something, he was looking at 15 years. He offered me a book about Malcolm X. I read it. It was a good read, and I learned a lot about this hero of ours. Schools spoke nothing of him. That's crazy.

I learned about Bullpen therapy. That's when the system sends you back and forth to court and nothing gets resolved, but you're annoyed at the suspense, the anticipation of it all. The willingness to take your lumps and run.

Or, get on with your bid, go to prison and start your journey. Hit the battlefield and pray you come out with the least scars possible. To live in insanity with the mind convinced of its normalcy.

Dawn was still my girl. We spoke on the phone and wrote to each other all the time. She knew I was troubled, but still gave me the time of day. I missed her, even loved her, but I was young and really didn't know what the heck I was doing to myself.

And even though I know my moms missed me, deep down, I think her mind was at ease, that I was at least safe. Plus, she knew where I was. I put her through so much already in my young life.

Lack of love was not the case here with us. I have a lion's ambition and if not properly or rightly channeled, I could destroy so hard. It's painful, a painful self destruction. All from within, this pain is hard to explain. God help me.

My public defender, I mean, public pretender was so fake. They would try to convince us that they were on our side and worked for the state at the same time. With your best interest in mind. "Yeah Right!"

It didn't take me long to figure it out. Despite me getting let off fairly easily. Standing before the judge was scary. This person could say a few words and your mind and soul could feel so destroyed.

My moms always had a sad, hopeful face in the courtroom. I realize now, I aint shit for putting her through that time and time again.

Judge gave me 2 years. This was a gift. The look of relief was clearly expressed on my moms face. She smiled, I smiled back, and told her I would call her tonight. All the while being marshaled out of the courtroom with my hands and feet shackled doing the shuffle.

Since I only had 2 years, I could do my time in the County without being transferred to the prison. I dodged a bullet. The County was sweet. You could eat in the dayroom, watch TV there, play cards sometimes, use the phone on the tier. Go to the courtyard and play basketball or just stand around and associate with the wrong people, have the wrong communication and sometimes, people would fight.

I got into a few fights, but they were mostly on the cell block or dayroom. And I can barely remember why.

I used to work out like crazy. Push ups, pull ups, dips. We had silent competitions going on. Most of the time I didn't realize how physically strong I was. Usually it showed when I had to punch somebody in the face or something.

Dawn thought I would be away for the whole 2 years. She was sad, but still mine. I didn't put much thought into my bid. All I thought was, I was in Long Lane for 5 years. That went by fast, so 2 years would be a good piece of cake. Wasn't a good way to think, but that's how I got through it.

So you couldn't imagine after only a year's time, maybe more, they popped my cell open and sent me to the property building. I didn't understand. I asked all the correctional officers "what was going on?" and all I remember is them saying, "what you don't want to go home"?

I said, yes, but I have 2 years. I only did one so far. They laughed, but I didn't get the joke. The CO said "is this your first time in jail?" Yes! Well come to find out, they had what's called, good time. And apparently, I accumulated enough to send me packing. They gave me $75 gate money, a pack of cigarettes and 3 condoms for the road.

When the gate opened up, I didn't believe it was real, but it was. I walked home, my project wasn't far from the jail.

I just walked into my moms crib like I never left. She was in shock, and my brothers and sisters were also. They clapped. We all cried and hugged. And I put some regular clothes on, and went to Pook's house. The family didn't want me to leave, but I said I'll be back and took off.

Tia opened the door, she hugged me hard as can be, and kissed me on the cheek. I didn't want this to happen, but I guess for being away, my body was doing its own thing. I got excited, I was embarrassed for having such a reaction. She understood, but didn't stop staring at it.

I hadn't smoked weed for a second, so, soon as I inhaled, my energy went somewhere else immediately. My body was tingling. Mind traveling. I couldn't believe I was home.

Tia handed me the phone, I was dumb struck. I said "hello", and Dawn was on the other end excited, but pissed off I didn't come over to her house first. But I explained my plan was to surprise her after school like I did before.

8 I'M WILDING

Ms. Cooper asked me if I would help them move. Of course I did. It was like 5 of us, it took 6 hours total. Afterwards, Ms. Cooper got us KFC.

They moved from Ann Street to Clark Street. Clark was the hood, but certain kinds of people could still maintain levels of privacy in their life. Depending on how they carried themselves.

And the Cooper family, I must say, had good character. I really extra loved Dawn's grandmother. I used to smoke weed with her, and sometimes played spades as her partner. She loved me. Plus, nobody could cook like her. Well, Ms. Cooper was taught by the best, so she was great in the kitchen also. But hands down, Dawn's grandmother was the best.

I could do no wrong in her eyes. She always had my back, no matter the situation and I loved her for that. Ms. Cooper knew in her heart how much her moms loved me.

I met Dave Cooper, Dawn's Uncle. He was cool. He used to hustle too. He moved in with Dawn's family for a while. Dave was hands down one of Ms. Cooper's favorite brothers. They had a pretty big family too.

Sometimes, Tony, Dave, and myself would be in Ms. Cooper's bedroom smoking weed and playing video games all day long. Dawn didn't mind because she was happy that I was at her house. I had clean fun there. No trouble, no risk, no danger.

She didn't want me to wait anymore, she felt she was ready for sex. Now I really thought the weed must have had me hearing things. Dawn never spoke so anticipatedly horny. What I think happened was, Tia being her friend, she probably told her that if she wasn't giving it up, that I would go get it elsewhere.

Tia was all in the business. She said, "Oh, my girl bout to finally get some huh? About time!" I wasn't trying to have that conversation with her, but she kept pressing.

I was twisted. Went home and talked to Dawn all night. She planned to skip school and wanted me to pop up at her house.

I couldn't wait. I ran straight to her crib, full speed ahead. She wore those tights she knew I liked. We started kissing. Like animals. She barely needed to come up for air. I was impressed. This was different, a great different though.

I was gentle with her and knowing that she was my virgin was a great feeling. I asked her, let me know when you climax. She really didn't have to say anything though. The way she trembled said it all, and the smile afterwards let me know it was a victory. She said, "let's do it again", and we both started laughing.

I didn't have any money so I was getting antsy. I went to see Bilal again. He was in the same position, same spot. Still crushing the game. It was perfect timing for me because Bilal just copped a new car and hooked it up. So really, he wasn't trying to be in the hallways all day doing business.

Since I was gone, he had been doing everything by himself. People just couldn't be trusted, and he knew that. I was getting the same split, 60/40, which wasn't bad at all considering I didn't have a dime to my name at that time.

That first week went well. As a matter of fact, it seemed business had picked up a bit. My $10,000 pack was moving in like 2 or 3 days, but I started spending less time at Dawn's and she was mad about it.

I was slowly but surely getting pulled back to the streets. I saw it, felt it, but couldn't stop it. I didn't want to stop it.

I made some new associations in my projects. This kid Wee-Chee, and Scott La Rock, and many more cats that watched me move about since I moved there. They knew me, but I didn't know them per se.

Wee-Chee was the wildest of the new batch I hung around. He always had access to the biggest guns. I wouldn't be with those cats full time though. I still had my job in the hallway on Main St. and this was steady income. They say, "if it aint' broke, don't fix it", and I wasn't.

Wee-Chee and the crew had crazy heart, but had no money. I had both, so it was said. Wee-Chee knew from an unrevealed source that I liked to do robberies. It wasn't really that I liked them, it was just easy and gave me a crazy adrenaline rush at the same time. Since I was a baby I have always been hyperactive.

The timing of this incident was crazy. I was just standing around the hood, having conversations with the locals when this Jamaican dude I met on the Wild Wild West in the Metals (the county jail) came through in an Astro van. Him and some other cat.

They wanted to rob this dude he knew on the other side of town. Really, I didn't want to get my hands dirty, I didn't need it. The dude kept bugging me and you know what they say, "be careful what you ask for."

So I hopped in the van. We went to Bowles Park, this project off of Blue

Hills Ave. Cats were standing out there deep, hustling. I made the gesture like I was smoking weed. This let them know I was looking for it. This fool left the herd and strayed off into the van with us. Big mistake holmes. We drove off with him towards Bloomfield, which was the next town over, but we didn't go that far. I pulled out my 380 on him, told him to run his shit. He had nowhere to run. Trapped.

He pulled out this huge zip lock bag full of weed, almost a pound, and like 40-50 bagged up dimes. I took that, and he had on a nice chain, bracelet, and a few rings. At first he tried to act like he couldn't get the rings off his fingers, but after I smacked him upside his head a little with the 380, they seemed to come right off.

I also made him take off his clothes right there in the van. All the way down to the underroos, then made him get out. But what I hadn't noticed was his boys from his block were following us in a black Toyota Corolla. The windshield was stomped in, and it had crazy bullet holes in the doors.

They scooped him up and got right on us shooting. I told the driver of the Astro van to step on it and not let them get in front of us. The light skin Jamaican dude got shot in the head, but he was alright. They kept yelling at me to shoot back at them.

They didn't understand my position though. I only had 3 bullets in my gun and I wasn't wasting them. I was saving them just in case we flipped over in the van and them fools wanted to make sure we were done. I would have faked dead then popped one of them and ran if I could, or if I had to.

That was my logic. They couldn't understand that. We got away and made it back to my hood safely, I guess. We hopped out the van and it was blood all over the place from this dude's dome. The van looked crazy.

This chick named Melissa from the project saw us get out of the van and had a bandana on her. I grabbed it and tied it tightly around this dude's bullet wound and told his people, "Yo, bring him to the hospital right now." but they wanted their cut of the shit.

Somehow they were thinking, since the dude got shot for the merchandise and his moms van was not only shot up with holes, but ruined with blood all over the place, that they should get all of it. Nah. I gave them the bagged up dimes and the broken gold chain. I kept the half pound of loose weed and the bracelet and rings.

They left the project mad as ever. I told them I didn't want to do it in the first place. "See, be careful what you ask for. Check this, the dude who got robbed had the nerve to be wearing a lion's head ring with rubies for the eyes. Some kind of lion he was. I wore that ring and sold the others.

I went to Pook's crib and told them what happened. I brought with me 2 boxes of Garcia Vega cigars. We smoked weed out of them. The weed was fire! Some lime-lime with red hairs. Tia kept trying to get me to give her some for free. Hell nah.

That weed was free, but expensive.

She called up Dawn and handed me the phone. Dawn was so mad at me. I hadn't been over there in weeks, and even though I did miss her, love her, and wanted to go over there, I didn't. The streets had me in a headlock. I told her I was on my way right now and if she didn't believe me, call a cab. I talked with her until the cab pulled up.

I gave Tia a small draw of the weed for reminding me what was really important. I needed that reality check. Dawn was home alone, perfect. We had sex and just laid in her bad and talked like we were the only people in the world.

She cursed me out good, and I deserved it. She asked if I had another chick, I didn't. I really didn't and I told her that I was just open off the streets. I know she didn't understand me, but that's what it was. I was stupid. I thought the street life was exciting and the hard way was the only way I ever learned. I started to go see Dawn more often and every chance we got to sneak sex in, we did. If the family went to the mall, the corner store, her grandmothers crib, anywhere, we got it in.

I went to see Wee-Chee and the crew. They were fiending for some action. They were all selling dope in the projects and business was booming in that particular market, but they loved gunplay.

I found out that they were all gang banging. I really didn't see myself going that route, but I told myself, If ever, I would go with them. They were "Solidos", which means solid in Spanish. I know other people in other gangs and the way they moved was whack. Someone in position was always trying to manipulate his own people into doing their bidding, sell their drugs, handle their beef. Do their term in prison for them, etc.

Gangs were big on the scene at this time. The 20 Love consisted of mostly blacks and Spanish mixed. The Latin Kings, self-explanatory and the Solidos were majority Latin, but blacks were also mixed in.

Wee-Chee and them were all Solidos. The back of the project was run by them. All the dope sold or whatever money came through the back belonged to them. In the front, where my building was, 20 Love dudes usually conducted their business affairs. Solidos sold when and wherever they stood, period, and were way more organized in activities.

But on the rise was this new crew called "young guns." There was only like 8 of them at the most, but they were doing major damage in the streets of Hartford.

They had beef with 20 Love, and it seemed like every other day a YG was getting a 20 Love dude. And when I say getting them, I do mean killing them.

But it didn't make sense how such a tiny crew was getting the obvious best of this huge gang. And to make it even more weird, those YG cats were easy to find. They weren't hiding at all. They would be right out in the open selling drugs in their hood and waiting for it. But it hardly ever came their way.

Solidos mostly had problems with LK's. They used to be cousins, connected in drug trade and in being Latin. But all that went out the window when dudes started having sex with each others women.

Envy and Jealousy always sets in. Over in Dawn's hood I met this cat Hank. Dawn knew this Hank cat since they were very young. Her whole family grew up with his whole family and they all agreed that he was trouble. So when Dawn heard that we hung out suddenly, she was tight.

Hank was down with 20 Love. This cat loved to fight. He grew up in this huge project on the south end called Charter Oak. This was the largest project in Hartford. It's also where Dawn's family is originally from. When I was younger I was brought through there a few times.

My cousin Russell stayed there with his Puerto Rican family. They were good people too, I remember how they always wanted to stuff me. Calling me Flacito.

I started having people rent me cars for money. I would pay them to rent me cars in their names. Brand new shit. I would pay for the cost of the car and slide them 2, sometimes 3 hundred for themselves to take the risk with me since I didn't have a license. But money talks.

I got hooked on driving rented cars. Sure it was expensive, but it was a luxury I had to afford. Picking up Dawn was fun, she always begged me to let her drive. My line was, "baby, you don't even have your license," and she would respond "you ain't got no license either" and we would burst out laughing.

Dropping her off was always hard for me. She wanted me to come upstairs with her and hang out, but I always had some street shit to tend to. She would take the car keys and run upstairs with them. This guaranteed me coming up, problem. Once upstairs we got to kissing and talking, and more kissing, less talking.   Laughing.   Before   you   know   it,   I'm   asleep.

9 SLOW DOWN

I hung out in the back a few days with Wee-Chee and the crew. Watching them hustle dope and post up. Running up on cars, serving bags and bundles with gats on their hip. Even the Spanish chicks in the hood sold dope and got it in. It was fun to watch them.

And if you let them, they'll smoke up all your weed and catch all the sales on the strip. I had a rented Buick Skylark, brand new with the year joint. Everybody kept asking to drive it, but I couldn't. If somebody was going to fuck my movement up, it would be me. Not you.

Wee-Chee wanted me to bring them to get dust. This cat Tito-Tical had it on the Avenue. I didn't smoke dust, but I took them to go cop. These fools were out of control.

As I was driving; I did inventory of my surroundings. I had 2 guns on me, so did Wee-Chee, so did Scott, so did Russian Vic. And if it were up to us, this is how the crew should move from A to B.

Tito-Tical was scary; but had good reason to be. When we pulled up he was serving a bunch of people. By the time he came over to where we were, he was almost out of dust. He stuck his head inside the car, saw all those guns and told Wee-Chee he and the crew could have the rest of the bags he had left for free.

I could only hang out with Wee-Chee and the crew in small doses. The north end of Hartford was a tight dangerous place to be in almost every hood, but when I came through my hood, everybody was shook.

I started staying at the hotel. Sometimes at the Super 8, and sometimes at the Indian spot. The Indians were cheaper, but more exposed to danger. I was sitting in the Skylark sparking up when this cat approached me, not knowing what he had just got himself into.

Asked me if I get money.

Told me he was from the city and he had the best coke and best prices around. I told him "actions speak louder," and pulled out 5,000 just to call his bluff. We went to his room, he lifted up the dresser, and pulled out a bird wrapped up in duct tape. He asked what I was spending, I gave him the $5000 and he gave me back something crazy. Oh, he got my attention.

I took his number and slid back to the parking lot. Re-sparked, looking at the work I copped. That fool appeared again, hopped in his rental with a nice looking Spanish chick, hit the horn at me. I hit back. I was side by side at the light until he jetted in the other direction.

I had a crazy feeling that this so called city cat just made a scarecrow move. The housekeeper, dope fiend little chick named Lil Bit had her little cart and cleaning supplies. I bribed her and asked her to open homeboy's door. I went straight to the dresser, lifted that and you wouldn't believe what I saw. The rest of that thing I got served out of. "Wow," my lucky day. I hit Lil Bit off with a chunk, maybe an ounce of coke. She damn near fainted.

I hopped in the rental, and went straight to the project. I had basically gotten a key for $5000. I was still selling ounces for $600. That shit went in one day. I celebrated with a new wardrobe, got super fresh.

I went to this club on the avenue, Jamaican spot. Look who showed up with his entourage; the kid I caught for the coke. He accused me, and it seemed like the music had stopped. His people were holding him back, but if he got crazy I would've introduced him to the twins.

The dude Hank was a womanizer, I don't care if he was on the phone with a woman. He would put her on mute just to try his chance at getting another one, it would never stop. Even if they were excellent people, he didn't care.

So I could understand why Dawn didn't want me around a person like this. We still hung out though. This cat also loved driving, Even though he didn't have a car. Once you allowed him to push yours, he kept the keys hostage.

Sometimes, while I was on the block hustlin, I would let Hank use my rental and go get me weed, Mcdonald's, or whatever but this ungrateful cat would disappear for 3-4 hours and come back with no gas and a car full of people like this would be cool to me. All of them broke and expecting me to put more gas in the tank.

It was things like that that stopped me from letting him be around me. I paid for everything. Every now and then he'd bring an opportunity to the table, but they all came with heavy risks. Always. We robbed this dude for a few stacks and his jewelry, some expensive pieces and Hank kept it all.

Greedy was his middle name. We met this other stick up kid named V at the gambling house. Would you believe V was smart but stupid. He'd rob banks and get away with 20-30 thousand easily, but then on the same night, gamble it all away and be twisted until the next job.

Then keep repeating the cycle. I couldn't believe it. He wanted me and Hank to rob this check cashing spot with him. The plan was actually good. At this point I hadn't done stuff on this level, I mostly robbed drug dealers etc. not banks or any financial institutions but we pulled it off.

Even took the weapons from the so called security they had. It was the first of the month and the take was for 70 cash. We used my vehicle to get there, to get away etc. But somehow, my portion was the least. I only got $5000, even Hank got $15000. I was pissed. That was a first and last for me. Hank overdosed at the mall, spent his money like he was some kind of millionaire.

We met these girls. He was all into the one he was trying to sleep with but I wasn't on it like that. The other chick was pretty and all, but I had Dawn and I know she was a way better grade than that one. Hank brought these girls to the mall with us, showing off, he spent 85% of his money in that mall.

I bought a few things, but had other stuff on my mind. Hank still didn't pay for my gas, still didn't pay for the weed, but he did ask for my connect's number who rented the cars for me. I didn't give him the number he was pissed. We came close to fighting that night.

I had enough. I dropped him off at a chicks house and went to see Dawn. I told her I was going to kill Hank. Bring him in the back of a building to speak with him, then leave him back there by the dumpsters. She actually talked me out of it. Saved my life. I was going to do it and he never would've seen it coming.

Even the thought felt good inside. I'm bugged out!

I met this kid from the projects named Chin Chin, he was the leader of the Solido's. Chin Chin smoked dust. I don't know how the qualifications process went, as far as electing a leader but this fool was special. Chin Chin always had 2 guns on him. I don't care what time of the day or where you caught him.

He liked my style off the rip, he'd always ask if I was "ready for my colors." I just smiled. Chin was responsible for keeping the hood organized and on point. If dudes were making a certain amount of money, they would have to pay dues.

Probably like once a week, $50 or so. If you wanted to give up more that was on you. Dues real purpose was if one of them went to jail and needed help either bonding out, or, maybe just money to spend on living in jail.

But Chin spent them dues. Once he collected them, that was for his pocket. Chin had the authority to send cats out on a mission anytime he wanted or saw fit.

That's when you go out and smash something, by something I mean someone or one's. Mostly enemies if there had been. Usually it was enemies. One thing people respected extra about Chin and his position was that he didn't just send cats out to scrape. He would go out all the time. He loved it, and you could always tell when he went out the day after because he would still be wearing all black. He would also smoke that dust a little more heavily than usual. Chin was a psycho. I went out with him a few times even though I wasn't down with the team officially.

They would even let me sit in on their meetings sometimes. It was crazy. When dudes lost their colors and had to get terminated, it was an ugly sight depending on the charge they gave you.

They had rules and all that. There were penalties for violations.

Weeks later I saw Hank when I was leaving Dawn's house. She dropped something heavy on me, told me she was pregnant. I know we were young, and I definitely wasn't ready for that. I was super reckless, but still excited.

I couldn't wait for her doctor's appointments. Ms. Cooper sat me down and basically told me it's time for me to grow up. She said it to both of us, but I know she was really speaking to me. I was a fool.

So I forgot that I wasn't speaking to Hank, I let him hop in my rental. We smoked all day, my weed of course, he was broke as fuck still living off of those clothes he bought with the robbery money.

I let him hold my guns since I was the one driving. Some YG's were behind us at the light. I don't know what really started it, but Hank was opening the car door and talking shit to them.

The light turned green. I pulled off not thinking much of it, but then these cats were getting too close to my bumper. I had to speed up a little. Now we were at the light on Main and Westland, they were behind us trying to creep up on the side.

I told Hank, "don't sleep", and he lifted up. Almost face to face with these cats, both sides dumping, bang bang bang, bang, bang bang. At least 30 shots or better, back and forth. I thought I would be hit once I saw the flash pointed right at me.

I took a hard left at the light, they took a hard right. I went to this project called The Ville. I hated dudes from the Ville, my project usually fought with theirs.

We jumped out in the parking lot to make sure we weren't hit, thank god, nobody hit. Almost never did Hank have good ideas, but now he did. He suggested we hurry and go to the movies to get stubs showing we were there, and not on the scene.

Since Dawn was pregnant, Ms. Cooper used to let me stay over anytime I wanted. And I slept in the bed with Dawn.

A few days later, homicide detectives came to Dawn's grandmother's house looking for me. Why they went there, I don't know; but they did.

Dawn's Grandmother Ree called and said the detectives were on their way to Dawn's house to come pick me up. Sure enough, they knocked on the door 5 minutes later asking for me.

In the streets, people called me JB because I got locked up at such a young age and for so long. It meant Jailbird. I wasn't proud of the nickname, but it stuck. So the detectives were looking for JB. They asked if I was JB, I denied it. They laughed and requested I come with them.

At the precinct, they already had Hank in a different cell and they let me know he was there. They showed me some photos and said, "do you know who that was," I really didn't.

Some dude in a hospital bed with all types of tubes hooked up to him and a breathing machine. They told me, YG's said it was my work. I couldn't believe they said that, but they did. Because other things the detectives spoke of that only those that were there that night could've mentioned.

Long story short, those YG's had big mouths despite all the shit they were doing in the hood. Hank held up, I held up. We walked out of there a few hours later. They even went to the rental car place and pulled some of the slugs out of the rented vehicle.

I had the person renting it for me report it stolen. Covered my ass.

10 COLORS

The heat was turning up in the streets with the gangs. All the shootings caused the feds to come in. Sometimes the GTF (Gang Task Force) would take over the block. Literally. Serve the customers dope and really pocket the money. Post up, and even push up on the chicks that would come through.

They took polaroid snap shots every now and then, to show who was who. And to have these groups as well as individuals on file. They would even let dudes hang themselves, meaning, flash their beads or tattoos, even do the handshake. Some cats just loved the attention, and really didn't know any better. Later, that would bite.

Since Hank was down with 20 Love, he was getting praised for the action that took place with the YG's. Rumors were, one of them got hit that night so people just assumed I was with that crew, which I was not.

Some so called, high ranking 20 love members had approached me about missing the meetings they held. I laughed them off, told them, "I'm not down with y'all", apparently they got offended. Heard there were rumors that spread that if anyone with the 20's saw me, anywhere, TOS. Which means terminate on sight!

Since Chin Chin was the head of the Solido's, people would give him hundreds of thousands worth of dope to sell. Knowing the projects was a gold mine for this, sometimes it would be 30-40 dudes out in the back selling dope. And in one day, they would all sell out what they had. This was daily. Money grew on trees back there.

So basically, all the brothers would get dope from Chin at a good price and all he had to do was wait and collect the money. He didn't even have to come looking for dudes, because they knew better than to play around with the money. Business was always good.

Chin sold me 2 boxes. Which is $10,000 worth. I paid 5400. In our hood, I could get that off in a few hours, early morning rush.

This kid from the hood, Green eye Ty, we never got along with each other, he used to box at Johnny Dukes in the projects. I heard he was nice when we were younger. I tried to knock him out but he was fast. So these days and times he was already down with the Solido's.

He saw me catch sells in the back, that was off limits for non Solidos. I knew better, but felt that since me and Chin was so tight, and he was the leader of them, I'm good. Green eye Ty didn't see it like that, he wanted me to give up my money. I didn't, I couldn't. So I pushed him and ran off. This was trouble.

Dope spoiled if you didn't sell it fast enough after it was bagged up and put through the repackaging process. So I still had to get my money. But very carefully. Green eye Ty didn't live in the projects anymore, but I did, so this was my advantage.

I approached Chin, told him I was ready. He was excited for me to come in, but had to check on something first. He went to the leader of the 20's and asked how we could solve the problem concerning JB. They wanted blood. They requested to terminate me, and after that, everything's straight.

When Chin told me that, I didn't understand it. I wasn't down with them, and now, they want to terminate me. To cut me loose. Chin told them he had to be present at the termination. And afterwards, he had my back to the end. It was agreed, but I was scared.

The location was behind the building I used to hustle for Bilal. I pulled up with Chin. They were deep as hell waiting for me, like 20 of them.

I gave Chin my guns, told him, "hold me down", this was crazy! I stood in the middle of them, someone said "Go!" and they started punching me, mostly in the face. Tried slamming me, but I knew if I fell they would stump me to death, so that wasn't happening.

This dude named Goldie pulled out a huge knife. Stabbed me in my face. Chin popped a few shots in the air, "Enough, Enough", they scattered. It was over with.

I could barely see. Blood was all in my eyes but I made it next to Chin. Asked for my guns. I was looking for any one of them dudes to be there. Everybody jetted.

I left my car where it was and walked to my building. Blood was everywhere on me. My brothers and sisters saw me and were screaming. The ambulance was called.

When I got to the hospital I was good. They gave me red and blue stitches on my nose. That's where I had been stabbed.

GTF came to the hospital to speak with me. Told me they knew what happened and who stabbed me. Then they asked If I wanted to press charges. "Hell no.

I don't even know what happened," they laughed and said, "suit yourself, let us know if you change your mind."

I fell back a few weeks to heal. Spent time with Dawn. She was pissed at me. She kissed my ugly face and made me forget I was injured.

We went to the doctors together for her prenatal pills and some counseling on parenting. It felt good to do that. Regular human being stuff. I wasn't used to that. Normal was weird, crazy was regular. "I need help!"

I met up with Chin in the projects, we spoke briefly about what happened that day. He saluted me, said, "that was crazy." My scars were almost unnoticeable.

Chin made a few calls, and we got set up in the graveyard. Today was the day I took my oath, seemed like the whole project was there.

I didn't know about initiations from other families, but this one, you had to bang in. Meaning you have to fight 2 dudes at the same time for 2 minutes. Everything goes. Punching in the face, kicks to the nuts, Whatever.

2 dudes from another hood were the ones I had to bang with. It made sense. People you weren't hanging out with every day in your hood were used to bang in, to show fairness.

Had it been my people, maybe they would of went light on me, or even faked it, just to let me in.

One dude was a giant, the other short and stocky. They were high, I saw it in their eye's, that boosted my confidence. Chin said, "Go!"

I focused on the big one, he swung wild trying to take my head off. I old school kneed him in the nuts. Me and the stocky one boxed it out, blow for blow until the 2 minutes was up.

The brothers chanted, "Solid, Solid" and I was in. The giant brother who got injured was still twisted. I felt bad, but really would have felt bad if he would have connected.

We celebrated in the projects. I bought weed for everybody. One of the sisters, a Solida, wanted to fuck. All the sisters pushed up on me, competing to see who would get me first. But they all lost that competition. My plans were bigger.

Dawn called me. She needed to see me AYAP. When I got there, it was a bad vibe. Ms. Cooper was crying, even Mara, Dawn's sister, was sad. I've never seen that.

Dawn had a miscarriage. She was at her grandmother's arguing with her uncle Brucey. I heard it was intense. She felt pain and had to go to the hospital. They automatically checked on the baby's heart rate, there was none.

Whatever medication they gave Dawn had her twisted. She was crying and laughing at the same time. I was pissed. After she told me what happened, I wanted to blast her uncle Brucey, Ms. Cooper knew.

I stayed with Dawn a few days. We talked, she seemed alright. When I got back to the hood, it was business as usual. Green eye Ty appeared. He didn't know I had my colors. I made it my business to catch sales right in front of him. Big sales.

He ran up, "didn't I tell you, you couldn't?" That's when the Q-45 pulled up. Everybody knew that was a crazy sale, but everybody was waiting for Chin. He got more dope last night, but didn't pass it out yet. So nobody had it but me.

The white dude Gotti in the Q-45 wanted $3000 worth of dope and $2000 worth of coke. I had both.

Green eye Ty was mad about it! I stood there counting money in his face. "If looks could kill."

I told myself, when I catch this dude somewhere away from the hood slipping, got him!

My cousin DOGG was down with 20 Love. He was younger than me, but very popular amongst the fools, as I called them. DOGG had a little crack crew, they were the ones selling "ready rock" in the hood.

Their spot was on Earl St. This kid Grady had the crack house. Actually, it was his moms crib. She got high also. She started the trend of cooking people's coke up in the microwave. Started an epidemic.

Dogg's Crew were kicking but when it came to selling crack, nonstop traffic. All day and night. Their block was a planet in itself. I felt entitled to get a piece.

DOGG's mom, my cousin Stacy, had an apartment in this 2 family house. She knew what it was, and DOGG was her pride and joy. He could do no wrong in her eyes.

Dudes were making so much money on that block, and they were all compulsive gamblers. They would roll dice and bet on the side all night. Since Grady's crib was the crack house, all the money would come straight to them.

But Earl St. was right next door to the Village, and this project had some enemies of mine in it. These were the dudes that jumped and stabbed me, but I still got my shit off on that strip. I always had 2 guns with me.

Still was suicidal though.

Back in the square, my projects, my downstairs neighbor on the 3rd floor was this lady named Alice. She had like 4 kids, I met her son Nate and instantly became his big brother. Light skin cat with red hair and freckles. Good dude. Respectful

People were allowed to hustle out of his moms crib with her permission. She just wanted a cut. This didn't benefit Nate one bit. But we fixed that right up.

I gave him a $2000 pack of crack. Told him to bring me back a stack, keep the other stack for him. He took over his spot. Kicked the outsiders out and looked out for his moms to an extent.

I know it wasn't right, but I introduced him to guns. First, I would have him stash them for me until I needed them. Then he started testing them on his own. Shooting at targets and shit. After a while, I gave him one. This young cat was loyal.

I could never forget the day I got jumped and stabbed. And, I knew specifically who held that knife. I didn't go on a hunt because I had a feeling this person would be hand delivered and gift wrapped one day. This day had come. I was hanging around the hood with a few brothers, just smoking weed and enjoying life until I looked at the red light and saw something special stuck in traffic.

My lucky day. It was the cat that poked me. I tied my red bandanna on my bald head, ran up on the caddy, and opened the passenger door. You should've seen the fear in this sucker's eyes, placed my piece directly on his skull, squeezed on him. After I got him, the driver sped off. I kept squeezing the automatic. Dropped the back window. Bullets bouncing off the car, finally jammed my joint. I ran off.

4 old ladies were sitting right there, and had a front row seat of the drama. Looked right at me, in the eyes as I got ghost.

I went to hide the gun at Nate's, he watched it all unfold out of his window.

11 DAMN

Me and the crew had a good laugh about my little episode. But unfortunately I was given bad news. It seems the dude I plugged was actually up and about. I thought he was hit in the face, but apparently I got him in the upper chest and around the neck area.

Either way, I got even. My brother Taki, who I hadn't spoken much about because we lived totally different lives, had just moved to job corp in Mass. I was proud of my older brother. He went there to get a trade, to give himself a better chance at beating the odds.

While he was there, I guess he was getting the attention of all the bad chicks up there. Dudes were jealous that he bagged this Spanish girl named Maria from the Bronx. Maria had a crazy big butt. Anyway, he also had this other Spanish girl named Rebecca. Turns out Rebecca was gang banging. She was a so called "Queen".

Her fake brothers was pissed off that out of all the dudes in their family, who obviously wanted to be with her, and she still chooses this dude. Some regular cat who didn't live the life.

Job corp gave their students passes for the weekend to go home. Kind of like college students getting time off to blow steam. Taki used to come down on a greyhound bus. Even though I was heavily in the streets I enjoyed talking with Taki about his adventures there.

Ms. Cooper let me move in. It felt good to be able to sleep in the bed with Dawn. I'd Wake up in the middle of the night, looking out another window without seeing the projects, looking like a prison with all the bars on the windows. Sometimes I felt trapped, like this was the only place to be.

I was back and forth to Earl St. It was booming and no one was around, so I would catch all the sales and then head back to Dawn's to put my money up. Then bring more back to the block, over and over again.

Dawn stopped me right in my tracks, told me some bad news about Taki. She said, "he was at the hospital right now, he got stabbed."

I couldn't get to the hospital fast enough. When I got there, they were working on my brother. Pulling shit out of his neck, talking doctor talk. It seems some people followed my brother home from job corp, caught him slipping and sliced his throat from ear to ear.

Almost killed my good brother who was trying to be a better man who didn't do crime, sell drugs, do drugs, hurt people, none of that. And here he is. Getting stabbed up by some gang bangers.

They let me in to see him. He could barely speak, but told me enough to know what happened and where they might be at this very moment.

I went straight to the bus station. I didn't even drive there. I ran. There was a bus going to Bridgeport, oh yea, my brother told me these cats at job corps was from Bridgeport.

Without a ticket, I boarded the bus. The driver tried to hold me back, but I pressed forward like a demon. The people sitting already were startled, I looked for any sign of young people, and Spanish. I saw these two cats sitting together, tried to bait them, "Yo, y'all came from mass? Yall in job corp?"

If it was them, they didn't bite the hook so I left the bus before the cops came. And believe me, they were on their way.

That night I was on edge. I hadn't been home since Dawn gave me the bad news. I know she was worried. She knows I love my brother. Despite me being around seldomly. Just like with her and the rest of the people I love, but they know I love them.

"The freaks come out at night", okay. Tonight we were all out in the projects. I told Chin what happened with my brother. He automatically offered to go to mass and visit job corp with me. I respected the offer, deeply, and appreciated it. But I wasn't crossing state lines. I had a thought, and just then, this kid Highpower and Baby-us pulled up. They were Solido's also, but from the south end of Hartford.

They wanted to get busy. Go on a mission. I hopped in the car with them and told them my vision. Baby-us said he knew "the perfect victims," they kings too. Great!

We had Highpower wait like 3 blocks away with the car running while me and Baby-us cut through some back yards and crept up on these Latin Kings gambling. They had their beads on and all that. No mistaking who they were repping at all. I was glad for that, I felt nothing at all.

Baby-us had 2 guns, and I had 2 guns. We ran up and I yelled, "Amor de Rey" which got their attention immediately. Started popping them up on that porch, bang, bang, bang, bang, you get my drift.

Seemed like we were shooting for minutes. There were 3 of them on that porch. Like I said, there were 3 of them. Heart racing like crazy.

Got back to the car, Highpower wheeled us back to the North end, we reloaded. That mission was mine, now Baby-us wanted the North end. He wanted Nelton Court, the projects where I first got my hustle on.

Before we got there, I told Baby-us, "yo, my little sisters be hanging out with some girls there. So please don't squeeze on no girls, and also, I wasn't cool with hurting women, no innocent people period.

I had enough of that in my youth. No more innocent people.

So as we were pulling up Nelson Street, there was a group of girls standing deep at the entrance of the projects. I watched Baby-us, he leaned out the window, pointed at the girls and everything got quiet like we were in slow motion or something.

Baby-us pulled the trigger, but he didn't have his shit cocked back. Thank God. So his shit didn't go off. We kept rolling up the street, those girls were staring at the car until we got out of view.

I started cursing Baby-us out, "didn't I tell you, my sisters be out there with their friends?" He started laughing, I put my guns to his head and he cocked back and put his to mine. We yelled a little, then calmed down. "Yo, drop me off. And oh yea, burn this shit." Meaning the car.

I got a hotel room that night, just wanted to fall back and think and smoke like a chimney. And watch the news.

I just couldn't believe someone had hurt my brother, and almost killed him at that. The world is cold, even in May. Dawn beeped me, wanting me to meet her at Hartford hospital. First thing in my mind, "what the fuck, I can't take another tragedy in my life."

She hugged me super tight, this worried me. Then she smiled and grabbed my hands. "Pregnant!" I was numb for a second. "What did she just say?" She kind of knew for like 3 months, but since the miscarriage, she couldn't get her hopes up high so easily.

She actually was there for a doctor's appointment so we got the ultrasound done and talked with her doctor about how we could have a healthy, safe pregnancy.

My life was crazy. All drama. I took Dawn to the mall, bought her some lunch and went to lunch in the food court.

Her mother already knew she was pregnant, she just didn't say anything. "Oh." Dawn had gotten her license so every chance she could, she was trying to take my car. And since I only had rented cars every day. I always had the latest shit. The fast shit.

Dawn was taking the car to school a lot so I had to get rides from people at certain hours of the day. The dude Gotti came through, I was serving a lot of dope when the state troopers rushed in. Pulled up right next to us, I was still grabbing the money through the window.

I jumped off the state troopers bumper and hauled ass. All I kept thinking about was my guns. I knew they were dirty, and couldn't get caught with them or I'd be down for the count.

I didn't understand until later why they had a camera crew filming the raid. As I was running, my heart raced faster than my legs were moving. I couldn't stop thinking about my guns.

So for distraction, I threw the stacks of dope I had in the air in hope they would focus on that, while I got away with my guns. It worked. I made it to the back of the projects and ran into someone's open door.

They knew me, but it still was crazy. A Spanish family, they loved me. Cops and troopers were looking everywhere for me, I gave one of the dudes in that apartment the guns to hide and turned myself in.

I saw that they had the dogs out and it would be a matter of time before they found me. I couldn't let these good people get in trouble over my shit. Plus, as long as I didn't get caught with the steel, I'm straight. I was willing to eat the drug charges. Actually, since I threw them on camera, that case would be open and shut.

They slammed me on the ground even though I surrendered. First words , "where are the guns," to which I said, "what guns? I don't know what you're talking about."

Even the troopers admitted when they had me secured, cuffed in the back of the cruiser, "that was a very strategic move you made back there, throwing that heroin."

"You got away with the guns. We knew them guns were dirty. We get all types of complaints about you out here. And they come from gang bangers." I believed them.

12 OPERATION

No Morgan St. jail this go 'round, I went straight to the metals. My bond wasn't high, so they had me in the dorms. The dorms were wild, wide open all day and no privacy except in the shower. Same drugs on the streets, same ones in the jails. Just more expensive.

Dudes kept calling me to watch the local news. Apparently I was the headline all day long. They were slowing the tape down, saying "you can see the suspect actually throwing heroin at the officers." It did look crazy, I admit. They were calling it operation sweep.

I had a feeling the dude Gotti was a fed. He looked too strong and clean cut, and dressed way too sharp to be doing as much drugs as he was purchasing.

And, how come he wasn't arrested along with us? They rolled in the midst of a deal, and I did actually serve him. I wasn't the only one they grabbed. Scott la Rock got bagged also, and his face was on the news too.

They were calling it a gang drug sweep, but my charges weren't serious at all. Possession charges and resisting.

I went to court the next day. The courtroom was packed, almost the whole hood was there. I shouldn't have thought of this as a light matter, but being I didn't get caught with the burners, I had no fear of the outcome.

Nothing happens too much on the first court appearance. Usually just arraignment, basically, sorting out what category the case or cases might fall in.

Got a continuance for 2 months. I called Dawn every day and continued to commit crimes, even behind the walls. I still smoked weed all the time. There were lots of gang fights and so much other foolishness you wouldn't even believe.

I called Nate from jail, He was doing good. Told me he had a little problem with this kid Tyvon Martin, Tyvon was his next door neighbor. He was older than Nate by a few years, seems he was jealous that young Nate was eating and he wanted to eat.

Told Nate he was going to rob him, he had no idea what Nate was trained to do. They fought, Nate beat his ass. End of story.

The next court appearance a public pretender was assigned to my case. The prosecutor wanted me to take a plea deal; 2 years suspended after one year. Which meant, I would really have a year to serve.

But we had good time in the system, so I could more likely be out earlier than a year. Dawn was already 5 months, so I'm cutting it close. I took the offer that day quickly before they changed their mind.

I did another 3 months and got off on this stuff called SHR (Supervised Home Release), which we called, Soon He Return. Dawn was 8 months and I tried doing something different. I got 2 jobs, working in warehouses. Yep, 16 hours a day, working. I was trying to make Dawn proud of me. She knew this was out of my element.

I started buying things before the baby came. We were told we were having a girl. My vision was true. When I met dawn, I told her one day she would have my daughter and it was really happening.

I was copping all types of stuff for my baby. It felt the best. Our rule was, if she had a boy, I would name him and if we had a girl, she got that. We already had her name.

We did get a scare, and had to rush to the hospital. She was having contractions, but it was false labor. Doctor made us stay overnight just to make sure everything was good.

After a month, the job wasn't working. My boss at the second job was jealous of my energy after a big shift and started being rude. I checked him as soft as I could, but the next day I came to work with my gun. He never knew though, nobody did. Except one of my co workers. He was the one dude I vibed with on the job, Italian dude. He even picked me up for work, and dropped me off.

I'm so criminal minded. I had a whole plan in my mind that if my boss got disrespectful again today, I would smoke him, then rob the place for its petty cash. He kept it in the little office under lock and key.

Nate was climbing up the ladder fast. During that time I spent in the can, he made adjustments. The adjustments he needed. Found a new connect, did everything himself, still had my money and my guns. Didn't owe anybody money, didn't get hot with the police, and helped his moms out.

But he did become a gun fanatic. He purchased too many guns, like he was preparing for war. All the fiends brought their guns to him first. It was known, he paid top dollar, always.

Oh Yeah, he even had a little bucket. Shit he was living better than the average dude in the hood. And his moms didn't mind that his girlfriend would stay over a lot. He was helping with the bills.

Dawn beeped me with the, "meet me you know where." I probably was at the hospital before her. She was in labor for real this time. I laid in bed with her, holding her hand. Telling her how our daughter would be. She thought I was cray. Well, she knew I was, and still loved me.

I dozed off, only to be awakened by yelling and screaming. It was time. This Jamaican nurse was talking shit to Dawn, saying, "the baby ain't gon come out by itself." I checked her, She threatened me with, "keep it up, I'll kick you out the room."

Finally, I saw her head. Amazed! Then they pulled my baby out the oven. "wow, my Nasia."

Yo, she looked just like me already. I saw my future in her face. T'nasia Ward, I couldn't wait to sign whatever needed to be signed for that. She was all mine, no question about it. No blood test needed, my mind was blown.

It was crazy seeing that blood drop out. I played with the after birth, im nasty. They stitched Dawn up. I kissed her a lot when the nurse left. Told her, "thank you, I love you" like a million times.

Dawn was saying, "she's mine too" as if the baby was only mine. They brought my baby back to us wrapped up, "Im in love with her."

I called Ms. Cooper bragging about her grand baby, "she looks just like me," we even weighed about the same at birth.

I called my moms with the same news. Said the same words. She went crazy. My brothers and sisters did too. My baby was the first grandbaby on both sides, or so I thought.

One night not worth mentioning I was drunk and cheated on my very loyal girl and got another woman pregnant. I regret my disloyal act, but not my beautiful son that came about. His name is "Kamar".

Him and Nasia are three and a half weeks apart. God gave me both my kids as a gift, and even though my acts on earth thus far are terrible, I'm thankful for them.

It hurt Dawn really bad, finding out I had a son, and even more so that he was my first child. But time healed that wound. She loves him now.

I started hanging out again with Pook. He was a Solido too. He started going on trips buying ounces of dope and bagging it himself. Instead of buying it bagged up in stacks. This produced crazy more profit. He invited me to accompany him on a trip.

Out of nowhere, Pook had become this little pimp. He had this older Spanish chick, named Jada, from the Bronx. She put him on with the connect he had.

She came on the trip with us. He was like her little puppy. We spent $12,000, 6 each. Pook claimed he knew how to cut and package the dope. It was pretty good I guess. We gave out $1,000 worth of testers, just to introduce it to the hood. It got good reviews, "4 thumbs up."

So now, people are requesting our dope and a lot of people weren't able to make money like they usually did. Me and Pook couldn't be greedy and make all the money, somebody would tell. So we started copping heavy weight, selling everybody stacks now, instead of selling bags and bundles.

Now, we can't keep up with the demand. Soon as it comes, it goes. Which was great for us, but the people on the sidelines were getting tight. Even Chin Chin started frowning his face up.

One early morning, I was in the rental with Chin Chin talking about something big, while smoking weed. He watched me make $20,000 in 3 hours. He didn't speak on it, but I know his mind was wandering on what he was witnessing. Gave him $1,000 worth of dope for nothing. Just to brighten his day, then I watched him sell it. I Dropped him off at home, before I pulled off, he said, "yo, we gotta build later on."

Now Pook started getting too big for his own good. Buying Gucci links, big ass bracelets, driving big rentals. I always kept a rental, every day actually, but Pook was getting stuff that drew a lot of attention.

This little cat hopping out of big trucks, always counting money in the open for everybody to see him. He had like 10 kids. Fast.

Started hearing rumors that people were about to rob Pook, tie him up, take it all. I couldn't let that happen, not when I was his brother and partner.

But the people who wanted to get him were brothers. Other Solidos, dudes he wouldn't let eat. When they were in position he couldn't eat, and now he was returning the favor. But this was a dangerous move.

Pook was riding around with so much money, I even thought about getting him. Maybe, just to teach him a lesson.

That Jada chick, I knew would be trouble. We were at Pooks, counting money. Jada was there. We were about to make the biggest trip yet, and her diva came out crazy.

She told Pook she would make the trip by herself. We could relax and hold the fort down until she got back. Pook was trying to convince me to let her do it, "hell nah! I don't trust her like that." Now Pook wants to remind me that the connect is hers anyway.

She's the one that put us on, we can't eat without her. I knew it was over right then. I took my half of the money and was out. Pook and Jada stood there with their mouths open wide.

Jada was cursing at me, "you ain't nobody! We made you! I'm the one that put you on! Fuck you!"

2 weeks later, I noticed I was being followed. Had to be the cops, if it wasn't, something would have happened already. They tried to box me in at the light. I saw it a mile away, pushed that Mazda 626 like it was a Lambo. Got up out of that.

Cop jumped in front of the car, tried to smack him, missed him as he dove out of the way. I made it to the projects, like 8 cruisers were chasing me. Jumped out, almost dropped my gun. I Hid in big Jovanny's house. They had the dogs again. "They got me"

13 POOK

Heart racing, adrenaline up, High as fuck. Confused, angry, thirsty. Some of the things I felt at that moment.

When they put me in the cop car I was having an out of body experience. This cant be my life. Look who just pulled up, the cop I tried to run down. His name was Rivera, He threatened me for 15 minutes straight.

I didn't even know what I was arrested for. I hated when the cops were talking right in front of you, but acting as if you weren't there. And you automatically hate whatever music is on the radio, even if it was your favorite song.

On my way to the precinct I felt sick. I didn't know the charge, but I know it wasn't nice whatever it was. This time they took me to Jennings Road, another precinct in Hartford County. I was processed there.

They made me sit in the bullpen for hours, before they told me what the charge was. Which were, 1st degree murder, violation of probation, and evading. Oh, and resisting arrest. Which, why wouldn't I?

My bond was set at $500,000. I immediately got sober. Everybody gets one phone call. I made one, but I didn't want to.

I called Dawn. Hearing her voice made me want to cry. She did cry. I heard my baby in the background, check this, my baby was saying, "Da Da Da." The first time she ever said that, and what a terrible position I was in hearing it.

Dawn kept saying, "did you hear your daughter? She needs you, we need you." I felt like shit. Now I really didn't tell her what the charge was. I ignored her when she asked.

They took me to the metals. This time I went to the main building. Back on West-2, put me in the cell with this cat from DC, named Kev. He had a fed case, he was only in the metals to go back and forth to court. After that he'll be in the federal system.

He was a cool cat. He was in for robbing credit unions, he showed me his paperwork, all that. Big numbers. I didn't even know what a credit union was at that point. Kev explained.

He took $700,000 and was looking at 7 years. We talked a lot. Even though this cat was about to go up for a few joints. He was already focusing his mind on doing positive things when he got out. He still had most of that money.

He even made some clean investments. I was impressed.

My moms and Dawn were at my court appearance. I wish they weren't though. I didn't tell them what I was charged with, but all it took was a phone call, and that knowledge was public information.

The court room was filled with strangers, but it felt like everybody knew me. When they read off my charges the whole room got super quiet. Then, all you heard was whispers. I felt sad for my peoples.

The bond stayed the same, but really it didn't matter. I knew I was in for a long ride this round. They continued my case for 6 months.

I started getting my mind prepared for the worst possible outcome, and I didn't officially have my paperwork yet. Just the charge.

My moms came to visit me and she brought my kids with her. It was beautiful. They looked just like me and both had bald heads. They couldn't really talk yet, but their eyes told a story.

Kev was schooling me, telling me how to make my fake state lawyer bring me all the details of my case. How not to, let them just railroad me. How I had to challenge some things in that court. Basically fight for my life back.

Dawn came to see me. First and last time. She was such a good woman, and never did anything but stay by my side. Despite all of my madness, and continued madness. I had to let her go. She told me dudes were scared to say anything to her because they knew she was mine.

Nobody would cross the line. I can't lie, I kind of liked that, but I wasn't healthy for her life. And so, we broke up. She left crying, and I left the visit wanting to die. I was torn up inside. I just lost everything, or so it felt.

That night in the shower, I cried my pain away. I mean, it wasn't gone, but the tears helped me a lot. I had to keep all that inside. That hurt the most, but I did it to myself.

They called me out of the blue for court. It wasn't my date. When I got to the courthouse everything felt weird. The sheriffs came and brought me to a room where some homicide detectives were waiting.

They tried to get me to incriminate myself further, telling me, they know I did this and that. Just tell them what happened, was it gang related, etc etc. I couldn't believe these fools thought I was the one to be spilling the beans on myself. And stupid enough to think they would go light on me. "Nah." I denied everything.

But from the line of questioning and what they were asking about, they fucked around and unknowingly revealed their rat.

Only certain people knew certain things, or so they thought they knew the specifics. I felt better about my situation now. They were still fishing. So that meant to me, you don't got me. Not yet.

But I filed a motion of discovery with my public pretender. Kev said, they had to give me my file, entirely. And they did, after about 8 months.

My next court date was very hopeful, my pretender came with an absurd offer. Told me the state wants 55 years from me. I burst out laughing, the pretender wasn't expecting that reaction. He yells at me, "you think this is funny."

I told him, "listen, just give me the paperwork I asked you for. Don't deny me my due process.". Now I had his attention, now I'm speaking his language.

Got rescheduled again, finally got my paperwork. They tried to conceal the informant's name, but I knew who it was. They got nothing.

Now everything I saw my pretender I got more confident than ever. Trial. Trial. Trial. All I kept saying to him. And every court date, the offer would come down a notch.

Still wasn't low enough for me. The hood was like a soap opera and everybody knew each other's business. Word on the street was, Pook got caught coming back from the city with a lot of dope again.

Nate told me, but I was puzzled, what does he mean again? Come to find out, right before I got picked up, Pook got caught with something heavy. Him and Jada.

Now everything was making more sense to me. I took back my money when Pook got out of control, and didn't want to check his chick while getting our work on her own. They take the trip together, Bonnie and Clyde, get pinched, and told the cops about me.

They knew they were in hot water, so they needed to fry up a big fish. That fish was me, but it would all backfire leaving nothing but hot grease in the pan. No fish buddy, not I!

14 SURPRISE

They try to get people to take the plea, without them really knowing if the evidence would hold up in trial or not. Most of us, in a rush to get the court proceedings and bullpen treatment out of our lives, we take bad plea deals. The state knows we don't have faith in the system to be going to trial.

The stakes were too high this round for me, not to give my situation the full attention it required. My lawyer said, "12 years is the final offer." I thought about it for like, 30 seconds then shook it way out of my mind.

According to my gut and the questioning of those detectives, the rat had to be Pook. And I was willing to bet my life on that literally.

So, I told the pretender, let's go to trial. As a matter of fact, put in a motion for a speedy trial and I'll be going pro se. Meaning, I'll be doing the talking for myself.

He yelled at me, I yelled back. But when I left the courthouse that day, he knew, I knew, I was walking away from this shit.

They tried to sneak attack me and it didn't work. Last minute court trip, "accept or reject." Famous lyrics in the courts. I rejected

My pretender said, "today we start picking," meaning picking a jury. Alright, let's go.

Guess I was going to see if the state really wanted to play chicken, like cars, drag racing in the streets. Once they saw, I was really ready to pick, they sent my pretender to come talk to me.

He said, "5 years. You can't get any better than that." I laughed. His cheeks got red as fuck, "tell them, I'm willing to take 18 months right now, time served. I walk out the court today. Take it or leave it.

See, my guilty plea is really a weak ass win for the state, but nevertheless, a win. Why? Because this still goes on my permanent record. Basically, a stain.

I was antsy waiting for the response. They left me in that holding cell, almost right before the court closed its doors. The sheriff's came to my cell, ice grilling me, and brought me to the elevator, I didn't understand.

You only take the elevator to go to the courtrooms. I thought the court was closed for the day already. The pretender stood there, looking like he was about to get arrested. The judge came out, the stenographer, and a few other people whose titles I know not.

The judge gave me a quick scolding, then granted my wish. I plead guilty to manslaughter in the 1st. 18 months, time served. Free to go! "what the!"

I walked out of that empty courthouse with jail clothes on and roared like a lion, right in front of it. "AHAHAHAH! Motherfuckers!"

15 NICE TRY

First stop, Dawn's. I walked over there so fast! Felt like I was floating. Couldn't get up those stairs fast enough. I wanted to just walk in, but I've been gone over a year. So, I thought it would be disrespectful, so I knocked.

Ms. Cooper opened the door, she put her hands on her mouth like she was yawning. She stood to the side, body language told me to come in. "Yo", Nasia ran straight to me crying, she said, "Daddy."

I picked her up and kissed her. Hugged and kissed her some more. She was so big and beautiful. I was twisted! Then Dawn came out of her room. She had a look on her face like, "wow, how the heck is this possible?" I couldn't believe it myself.

This had to be a dream. A good one. The best!

I asked Dawn if I could stay there for the night? She let me. Even though we weren't together anymore, my clothes were still where I left them, hanging up in the closet. I didn't understand that one.

I took a shower and changed my clothes. Ms. Cooper cooked a great meal. Like always. After dinner, Tony, Ms. Cooper's boyfriend, asked me if I wanted to smoke a blunt. He knew I did, but asked anyway. Like maybe I quit or something, yeah right!

He asked me what happened, I told him, "honestly, I don't know."

I was watching my baby eat her food mind blown. She was smiling at me, food all over her face, pointing at me saying, "daddy." I caught Dawn staring a few times. It was innocent.

I held my baby in my arms until she fell asleep. She kept putting her little fingers on my face. It felt good. I smiled every time and watched her sleep. Ms. Cooper grabbed Nasia and put her in the bed with her. It was cute, she said, "come on, Grandma Baby." Tone gave me a joint for myself, and went in the room with Ms. Cooper, smiling like a devil. Me too.

I was on the couch, setting it up right with the blankets and a few pillows. Dawn said, "come smoke with me." We ping ponged the joint and talked. She let me know, "you're not my man, I'm single." With the saddest face, I told her, "I know that," and smiled.

Then I rushed her, rubbed her ears with my fingers, pecked her lips softly, then put my tongue in her mouth, enjoying her spit. Her nipples were hard through her shirt, I ripped it off her, Gave her perky breast CPR. She arched her back, I squeezed her ass tight. I could feel her trembling, she was nervous. She kissed me back violently once I got inside. Scratched the shit out of my back with every stroke. A minute later, all giggles like a little girl. We laid there, smiling, kissing, and holding hands.

She slept like a baby. I stayed up thinking, what should my next move be, and could I restrain myself from seeing Pook?

My family went wild when I walked through that door. We talked for hours. They all wanted me to stay in the house. So I did all day. We ate ice cream and watched New Jack City.

My son's mother Kim, all of a sudden disappeared. I went to her supposedly old work place, old apartment, nothing. I wanted to see my son. I didn't have a relationship with Kim, but I needed one with my son. He was beautiful,

1000% mine.

Dawn let me see the baby anytime I wanted. That was cool. I only remember taking her with me a few times though. Chin got locked up, but it wasn't anything serious. He'll be back. Nate was still getting money.

I still had a few dollars, so I started going to the studio. They had one on Main St. next to Nelton Court projects. It was called, "studio 10." It was actually in the back of this laundry mat.

They had professional equipment, good engineers, and the sound quality was excellent. They used to give me deals on studio time. My cousin Day Day used to rap too. So we formed this two man group, "The wickedest and The Rawest."

I can't remember who came up with the name, or who was who as far as the title, but people loved our music. We actually sold it all throughout the city.

My cousins, Dogg and Day Day were first cousins, their mothers were sisters. So they were tight. I started getting money on Earl St. again, but I didn't live with Dawn and her family anymore.

I started renting hotel rooms every day again. Mostly at the super 8, the spot was ghetto, but they at least had cameras and security. That kept fools from coming around.

A spot was started on Day Day's street, Center St. It was off of Albany Ave, they sold dope and crack, so I killed 2 birds by being over there. A lot of girls would come through, hoping to get bagged.

I met this chick named Cookie, real name Natasha Bailey, she was black and Puerto Rican. Great combination if you asked me. She looked like a cute princess with green eyes.

She lived on Florence St. right off Center, where I was hustling. I started off just buying her and her cousin Jessica food from the ranch house, then they wanted to smoke my weed up all the time. I told her, "I might as well just be your man," she smiled back, put her hands on her hips and said, "you might as well be."

I was on Clark St. hanging out with Hank, smoking as usual. Waiting for Dawn to get home, hoping to see her and the baby. It was getting dark, what the, Dawn walked up to her building with this dude standing beside her. I thought I was seeing shit.

Hank was smirking, messing with my head. It worked. I wanted to see if this sucker was going upstairs, he was, they were. Then I popped up. Walked in, "you, who you?" Dawn had this look on her face like "oh, shit."

The dude stayed mute, but I couldn't resist it. I pulled my gun out, smacked him upside his head, "bow!" Blood gushed out immediately.

Ms. Cooper ran up on me, said, "boy take your baby." I grabbed Nasia, she hugged me tight, then started crying, like she knew something was wrong.

I couldn't stand there, without finishing the dude, so I left.

I only drove around the corner, but I waited for this cat to come out. No way he was getting away. Hours passed, he tried to sneak out, Hank sitting around with me, waiting like it's a movie.

I waited for homeboy to get around the corner, "hopped out on him."

He took off. I aimed my gun at him, squeezed off like 12 shots. Tried to get him in the head, thank god I missed.

Then came to my senses, what the hell am I doing?

Dawn and Ms. Cooper heard the shots go off, they knew it was me. Dawn said, "did you shoot him?" I told her nah, he got away.

But don't worry, I'll let you go, you're free from me. I was serious. It was over now.

16 Cops and Cookie

I vowed within myself without words being spoken. Never will I again do what I just did, "unless it's out of protection for mine," and when I say mine, I mean any person I love. Period. I'll do anything to get my peoples out of harm's way.

I was on Center, feeling sad, hustling and smoking as usual. Out of nowhere, Cookie came through, asked me if I was alright. I told her what I just went through.

She hugged up on me, whispered in my ear, "you good." Then snatched my weed and killed it. What could I say?

My shift was almost over. I made like 2 thousand. I was about to go to the room and relax, walked to the bodega, got some cigars, gum, toothpaste, and apple juice. "What a combo right?"

Got back to the vehicle, look who was in that joint doing her toenails. Cookie, she had an overnight bag and all that. Told her I was about to be on the shelf, she told me, "don't talk about it."

Stopped real quick on the avenue, copped some more weed. Few things at the package store, and we was out.

What I liked at that time about living in the room, was, besides it being clean, it made my days seem like an adventure. I ordered a movie, no porn, regular stuff.

I ordered a pizza, blew Cookie out the frame and relaxed in bed. She went backwards to the door naked, when the pizza man came. She won that $50 bet. I mean the pizza man really won that.

It was some white dude, young. I stood behind her, smacking her butt while she was paid. Only to see the cat's facial expression. Priceless, he was scared to death.

We ate, then round 2, 3, 4, 5. Until we passed out. After check out, I had breakfast at Mcdonald's and dropped her off.

Scooped her an hour later, took her shopping. Hope she ain't thinking I'm a trick.

Called it another early night. Cookie was down again. This time, we fucked, then I took her to a movie. I couldn't really watch the movie. She kept playing with my dick.

I had to grab an empty popcorn can from the floor to bust in. Cookie cleaned up the rest, "I know, I'm nasty."

Back to the room, you know what, then check out. Dropped her again. Minus the shopping spree. Actually, I wanted to bring her to the mall, but if I did, she would always expect it.

So instead I gave her 6 dimes of weed and $200. Her eyes got big like, "what's this for?" I pulled off.

Her cousin Jessica started getting jealous, so she went clubbing with her that night. I went to see Nasia, brought her to my mom's to stay for the weekend. My sisters went crazy when they saw her.

She made the cutest, intense faces, and was always dancing. I wanted to show her off. I brought her over Cookie's house, dig this, I came with the stroller. It felt so different walking around with my baby.

Cookie's mom was on her, an older pretty Spanish woman, barely spoke English. Their house was super clean, and they had plastic on the furniture.

My daughter soiled her diaper and Cookie's mom rushed to change her. That was cool.

I strolled her back to my moms, it seemed like my sisters were waiting at the door antsy for me to bring my baby back.

I felt like I was smothering Cookie, so I didn't come around that night. The next day, we were in front of the house. Leaning on the car, hugged up.

When this, big lip gorilla pulled up in a little 190 Benz. He called her, "Cookie get over here." She looked stuck. I held her like, "hell nah." Homeboy was pressing up. I pulled out, I was just about to hit him up, when Cookie said, "No JB, he's a cop."

I ran off with my gun in my hand, heart racing. "What the fuck just happened?"

Pissed off wasn't the word, I was steaming. A week later, on a Friday night, I was driving down Florence St. Seen Cookie get in the car with this light skin dude, they pulled off fast. As they were driving up this side street, I pulled up on them, let them see my face. Aimed at the door, tried to hit the dude in the body while he was driving.

"Bang, Bang, Bang" just 3 shots. I don't know if I hit him, I didn't care. Peeled off.

A Few days later, I was at the weed spot on Mansfield Street, copping some smoke. Kid named Ruff Ron, was bragging that he had this bad chick, about to go to the room.

Swore I heard him say Cookie. Checked it out for myself. It was her, and Jessica was in the back seat with his mans.

So as Ruff Ron was about to hop in his whip and sail off in the night, I robbed him. Right in front of Ms. Cookie and her cousin Ms. Jessica.

Took his stupid gold chain, which I didn't want, his weed, let him keep his money, but I took his pride. Did him dirty.

Met this Spanish kid named, Hotty, he sold dope too. Also was a Solido. He told me about his connect, and offered me a partnership. I had second thoughts, my last partnership almost got me life in prison.

We put a few dollars together, got something big. He and his workers bagged it up. I just watched. It took a day to get done. I was tired.

One early morning, I was catching the morning rush money, and something told me to stash my gun real quick. I did, which was something I never do.

I was trying to serve this strong looking white dude fast, but he called me back, asked for my beeper number, so I stopped. Waited for him to write it down.

They came from all angles. They got me red handed.

Guess who the cop was running the operation? Big lip gorilla cop who was messing with Cookie. He smiled so hard, all you saw was teeth. Black Bitch.

17 WALKER

Back in the slammer. First couple of nights I was restless. My bond wasn't too high, but it didn't matter. Whatever might the sentence be, none of this was breaking me.

This was, nowhere near as serious as what I faced last round so I really didn't go at the pretender they assigned to me like I did before.

I had possession of narcotics with intent to sale. They didn't find the gun, oh, but they were looking. That big lip gorilla cop knew I had to have it close by.

I started off in the dorms, since my bond wasn't sky high, but after a few gang fights they wanted to seclude me from crowds of people.

My celly was a cool cat, named Cali. He used to be on the Avenue. As we talked day and night, seems we knew a lot of the same people. We both didn't buy a TV yet so, we reflected on the streets all the time.

He taught me how to play chess, use to beat the shit out of me almost every game. I think I won one in 3 months. We gambled 50 pushups for the loser, so I was getting diesel.

Cali's charges were less serious than mine, but I wasn't stressing it. I missed Nasia, and Kamar. I wondered how they were. I hated that I was a terrible father, but even so, I love them. "one day they'll know."

The back and forth to court thing was wearing me out. I had enough. The state wanted 3 years straight. I bit my bottom lip and took it. 3 year sentence. Caso cerado.

When the sheriffs brought me back to the holding cell, after I got sentenced, I sat and thought. But there was this kid, bragging, he was, "getting out of here today". He had weed on him. I took that. At first, he acted like he wanted to fight for it, until he peeped the posture.

Cali felt bad for me. I cried real quick, just to get those tears out of my system, then I was alright. 3 years out of my life. I was mad about it.

I surprised Cali with the weed I brought back from court. I had it wrapped up real good, but when I took it out the plastic it was in, "oh boy." It was enough for maybe, 9 joints. We didn't have EZ Wider or cigars, so we smoked bible sheets. The book of Matthew, it is what it is.

We were twisted in that cell. I started rapping and all that. Then we tried to play chess, but we just kept on laughing at everything. The correction officer chick was from Hartford, too.

She was ghetto as fuck. Her extensions were bad, and she knew that, but that didn't stop her from acting like a diva. She looked just like Martin Lawrence, we called her "Sha-Nay-Nay," then everybody called her that. She liked it.

Every time she did her rounds, she would stop at our cell. We were probably the only prisoners up all night laughing and talking. She knew we were high. The weed smelled strong as can be in that tight cell. We didn't care.

After breakfast, we sparked up again. The weed lasted for 2 days, and we got no sleep. The second day they popped our cell open, called me to the "bubble." Handed me some bags, and told me I was getting transferred out.

I knew it was coming, but I didn't think it would be that soon. I packed my little bit of stuff up, said peace to Cali, and was out.

I was going to Walker Reception Center in Suffield, CT. Anybody who had over 2 years and 1 day to serve, they had to go to walker for intake.

Gave me a little jumpsuit, and medical checked me out. Asked me a lot of health and personal questions, then sent me to my cell.

They took your sneakers, shoes, or boots, etc., stored them, until you left for the prison. Made you wear Skippy's or what we called, Karate shoes. They looked crazy.

You stayed in Walker for assessment, for like 2-3 months tops. Then you got transferred to a new spot. You in the cell 21 hours of the day. Got recreation twice a day, 1 hour and a half a pop. But often times the jail would be on lock down and you'd be lucky to get one rec a day for that hour and a half.

There's only 4 phones for like 60 dudes to use in that short span of time, so a lot of fights would occur over dudes trying to be greedy. Making 2-3 calls knowing the line would be long.

There's really like 120 dudes on each block, but they come out for rec. 1 tier at a time. First the top for an hour and a half, then the next tier 1 ½. Oh pardon me, I meant to say you're only getting an hour and a half daily each tier. So in actuality, 22 ½ hour lock down. Daily.

Everybody's in a hurry to leave Walker, get to wherever they have to go. Start their bid.

Everybody's rushing to get hot water before we lockup. We still got 30 minutes, but the line is long. And the water takes a while to get hot again. This dude from New Haven named Tiger, tried to pass me in line.

Short stocky dude. Light skinned. I checked him, "yo sun, fall back, you after me." And moved past him. He came towards me fast, I grabbed him by the throat and punched him.

His little buddies from New Haven were mad about it, I guess he was like their superhero or something. And then, they see him get handled.

I came to find out later, the dude Tiger got 100 years. But that's his problem.

3 months came and went. I was getting transferred to Enfield. Medium prison back in the days. Enfield was the spot to be in, as far as doing time. People got trailers, short for trailer visits. Your wife could come be with you for 2 nights.

This would be possible every few months if you stayed out of trouble. No fights, no tickets.

They still had trailers, but I wasn't eligible, plus you had to be married first.

Couple of dudes from the project were also in Enfield. Scott La Rock, few other cats. I guess Scott had a little juice card, got me moved to the same building he was in. G building I think.

Scott was a pure trouble maker, he wanted the whole world to know he was a Solido. He got me a job in the kitchen where he worked. I didn't mind, you ate a little better, and every now and then, you could drink soda. "Yay, right."

The LK's were playing the Solidos in baseball. Scott asked me to hold him down. I really didn't want to participate at all but Scott had a broken arm, so I went.

But I really didn't get it. On the streets dudes were beefing, bullets flying, people dropping, and now these suckers want to play baseball against each other?

Even though Scott had a broken arm, he still played anyway. He was up to bat, This kid from the other side of things was talking shit to Scott. He told Scott in Spanish, suck his ***k.

Scott aint do shit. I ran up on the dude, punched him in the face, his people attacked me. I fought like 3 dudes at the same time. I was getting one dude, but they still jumped me. They were weak, I felt nada.

Scott ran. Only one Solido stood there and fought by my side, all the rest ran. I was surprised, but shouldn't have been.

They took me to the box. I did 2 weeks there, then they raised my level to maximum security. I got transferred to Gardener C.I. in Newtown, CT. Hold on

18 FUCK YOU LOOKING AT

I went to Gardener looking wild. Fresh out the hole. Never dingey, but rough nevertheless. Regular procedure, intake, then medical. I was cleared.

While I was in the box, the prison Gang Coordinator tried to get me to admit I was banging. He knew the nature of the fight, just wanted me to admit it.

So its regular population for me. I was sent to B Block. Damn near the whole block were lifers. And I'm over there with my little 3 years. They had 2 tiers, just like Walker, top and bottom. They had universal weights in the middle of the block.

A ping pong table in this little room, and an extra tight basketball courtyard with barb wires blocking the skies full view. It wasn't that bad though.

It's a crazy feeling moving to a new block. Soon as you walk in, the appraisal starts. Cats is taking inventory of all your shit. Even your posture.

I was in the bottom tier. They put me in the cell with this dude from Bridgeport named Gringo. He had 30 years, but was still hopeful with his appeals. Told me his brother got life in the feds for their same case.

He was already down 14 at the moment. Believe it or not, this was one of the more cheerful situations in the building. I became nice in ping pong, time would fly in that little room, beating dudes down.

And I also started lifting the universal weights a lot, doing pushups and pull ups, dips, all that. My body was looking crazy. People told me, but I didn't want to hear that shit from no dudes.

Prisoners liked to play cards. Everybody swore they were the best. Spades was a favorite. I found myself gambling, playing partners in spades. Since I was new, and really didn't know anyone, I rolled the dice and played with this dude from Bridgeport, named Smitty.

At first, I thought he was plain garbage. The way he kept making foolish mistakes, especially when we were winning like crazy, but then I paid closer attention.

I stopped the game, asked the dudes I was playing against, "where y'all from?" They were all from Bridgeport. "I get it now." I was the fool.

They were rocking together. Out to get my money. Told them dudes afterwards that I owed, "oh yeah, that bread I owe, get it like Ceasar got Rome."

Fuck them cards. Then I had a fight over the ping pong table. Me and this New Haven kid in the courtyard. To be truthful, he won the fight, but I won the battle all day.

His punches were soft, mine were hard. He just got more off than me, but he had an entourage. Like 5 New Haven cats with life were there.

That didn't affect the outcome of the fight at all. I just didn't have friends on deck. I never really had one in my lifetime. Just associates. I'm good with it.

The reason I considered myself to have won the battle is because I'm alone in this jungle, and I remain me. The odds weren't in my favor, but I didn't give a damn, "I'm going in."

Its crazy cause, the same dude I had a fight with got jumped a week later by 20 Love dudes and knocked his furniture (teeth) out. I watched it all unfold from my closed cell door, that's right, closed.

When I saw that riot break out, I wanted nothing to do with it. And believe it or not, I felt sorry for the dude. I heard, the reason they jumped him was because he could box, and cats weren't giving him a fair one.

See, that's the reason I won the battle. I gave him a fair fight.

I heard the dudes that jumped him all got outside charges. So basically, they were already in prison, and they got charges that landed them a longer bid in prison.

I stayed working out, but I let a lot of my old activities go. I started writing music again and battling dudes in the ping pong room. Everybody loved that. It was live!

A prisoner has to do a certain percentage of his sentence in order to be eligible for a level reduction, meaning his security level to drop.

I got raised to the max level for the gang fight, and now they dropped me back down to the medium level. So, I was transferred again.

They sent me to Somers, which was in Somers, CT. This prison was the terror dome once upon a time. It still had a bad reputation of being a potentially dangerous place.

The cells were so tight, and dirty. It was hot as fuck, plus they had rats. I really didn't want to be there. The CO's would talk to you like you were nothing.

The rec yard was crazy big. Almost a thousand cats out there at one time. The rap battles were serious. You could really get embarrassed out there if you were whack.

The top rapper on the compound was flexing. "I sprayed em, played em, Muslim prayer rug, prayed on em."

I let him go first, the crowd got huge. More huge, then, even the CO's came to watch.

I let him finish. Then came in—

Yo, the years '89, I'm headed to prison/
Despite all the good advice, I still aint listen/
Stores hot, got burned in the kitchen/
Penitentiary fliction, cats getting killed for snitching/

2 years flashed yep/ back on the set, back on the steps, wit a pack, back into the wrong shit/
Should have been in the Pocono's, I'm fucking with Solidos/
Lil Pook from the projects, damn you nosy yo/

Called me Assesino, was in the streets clicking/
Out of control, not to mention, out on parole/

Enter the chow hall, food down, how y'all/
Posture of a general, snuff you send you to medical/
Its rules to balling, so when the cops call travel/
Be prepared when the black reeper bangs that gavel/

I ate the full clip, marinated in hot sauce/
Don't get you bun dipped in ketchup thinking you hot dog/

Repressing my anger, driving off fantasies/
Wow, what pat of earth will my millions of fans be/
Getting released from the cage, like being reborn/
Getting off on the mere thoughts, my people seeing me on/
Thoughts distorted, Demon, I fought it/
In a land not my own, but, I can't be deported/

His career was over, I'm the new shit. Now every time I hit the rec yard everybody want to hear something. My confidence was significantly elevated.

I wrote a few albums, stayed away from the gang stuff. Especially after dudes showed me their true colors in Enfield.

Time was flying, I was getting transferred again. This time to a level 2, which is a pre-release, minimum security joint. A place called Willard.

It was wide open. Ping pong in the middle of the dorm, which I wasn't touching. Basketball courts, track, volleyball court, handball court. I'm surprised you couldn't play golf there.

People were going home left and right in this place. Weed was everywhere, I could've smoked if I wanted, but I so called, tried to slow down. I really did. Even told myself I would get a job, any job.

Even shoveling shit would've been better than being in prison.
3 years went by fast, "I'm out."

19 A FOOL IS A FOOL

Back on earth, of course the family was happy to see me. They always were. I love them. Dawn brought Nasia to me at my moms. She is growing up so fast.

She's extra smart, and beautiful. I know it's easy for any parent to say this about theirs, but my baby is really those things I said.

Her love for me is the strength of my life. Even though I haven't had the equal opportunity to spend time with my son, he's also my heart. The love you have for your son is different than your daughters.

My son is not only my twin, but he's a young lion. A Tonka truck, he could run your ass over and keep going without a scratch, without breaking. He's going to be a king one day. It's his living birthright.

Nevertheless, the guilt of me being a bad father weighs in. God willing I will grow up soon.

I felt like Hotty owed me some money. Before I got bagged, we made a substantial purchase of dope. And all I was hearing about while in the can was, how Hotty is eating out there. He has this project on smash.

Everybody's working for him. He's driving this, and that.

He's got the best product. He's making all the money. It didn't bother me to hear those things, but knowing my money is invested, I would hope Hotty doesn't develop amnesia.

Especially when I know, a gun upside his head, should refresh his memory. I didn't want it to come to that.

Hotty lived on Florence St., the same street Cookie lived on. I went to his old apartment building. His family still lived there, but said he hardly comes around to visit these days. I understand.

I'll catch up with him one day. Hartford is only so big. I saw this very attractive Spanish young lady, sitting on the stoop outside of this very popular apartment building.

I investigated, introduced myself, she obliged, her name was Kathy, but her people called her Kit Kat. Like the candy bar. Told me she was single, I found that hard to believe. I wanted to know more about her.

I always maintained an appropriate appearance. I wasn't hustling at the time, was trying not to. When Kathy allowed me to speak with her, I told her the truth. That I hated living the street life all of a sudden. I keep ending up in prison. The job search was frustrating, being that I didn't have an impressive work history, or a certified trade or skill to fall back on.

But I got on that bus, filled out those applications, and humbled myself in hope to land a job. I was trying. I was getting the impression that Kathy was hoping for a street dude. We used to be on her building stoop, and then drug dealers would zoom by with their nice cars and music blasting. This would steal away her attention, every time.

It made me feel like shit, only because I knew. Whatever those dudes were doing, I've been there, done that, and could easily fall back into that lifestyle if I chose.

She wasn't my chick or anything, not even mt friend. Really just someone I was getting to know. I hadn't kissed her, had sex with her, none of that.

We had plans to smoke weed and talk later, nothing major; but I was looking forward to it. Anyway, soon as I got to her building, her and her girl Smiley was hopping into this Spanish dude's ride. If you could see the happiness on Kathy's face, while squeezing into the back of that car.

She didn't see me, but I saw her. I was heartbroken. Only because she could have just told me she had plans. It still would have hurt me, but I would've understood. I made eye contact with the driver of that car. You should've seen the arrogant smirk on this jerk's face when she got in.

I wasn't visiting Kathy anymore, there was no need.

I was downtown Hartford filling out applications when I saw this kid named Pablo. He was big at the time in the dope dealing industry.

I wasn't trying to hear it, but I heard a lot of people speak about his work. Everybody wanted it. His stamp was, "Black Sunday." Very popular.

And so, I asked him for a shot. It took a lot out of me. As prideful as I considered myself, to ask this man for a chance to get back on my feet.

He gave me that shot. First couple of weeks went smoothly. A few people in the hood had dope already, but they didn't have, Black Sunday.

So soon as I appeared on the scene, nobody else could sell shit. Everybody was mad about it, kept asking me, where did I get Black Sunday from? Did I know Pablo and could I get as much as I wanted?

How Pablo did it with me, whatever I bought with my own money, he matched it on credit. It was a good deal for me. I wouldn't spend shit. No clothes, rentals, barely smoked weed, no hotel rooms, nada.

I needed all Black Sunday, and he delivered fast. Took almost a month, I hustled hard and saved up $15,000. Made my order with Pablo. He told me to hold on, he would send his right hand man, Claudio.

Told him to meet me in Sands. It was the project next door to mine. They were almost connected at the hip, right across from each other.

Meet me in the high rise parking lot, in the back by the train tracks. Since I was still a Solido, I utilized the status for my favor. Got a loaner A.R. 15, but it didn't have any bullets.

I didn't care, I needed it for intimidation only.

When Claudio came with the Black Sunday, I saw him park. He stayed in the car, waiting. I limped over with the A.R. 15. He rolled down the window, I stuck the A.R. in his face. Made him give me the keys and strip naked.

I took the shopping bag full of dope, his money and his big ass link. I think he had a few rings, don't remember.

After I grabbed everything, I looked into this cats fearful eyes. Yo guess who it was? Mr. Arrogant, watch me stuff Kit Kat and her girl in my dope mobile and leave you standing there.

The tables had turned. I returned the A.R. 15 and went to count my goody's in an abandoned apartment.

So I ordered $30,000 worth of dope. He must have had other deliveries to make because there was another $15,000, plus he had $10,000 in his pockets. His jewelry was extra, for the smirk on his face that night.

Plus, I still had my own $15,000 that I made the order with. All this was spur of the moment. I hadn't planned on this, but my demon was out. Kathy turned my demon on.

I wondered, what would it take to turn him off?

20 DIDN'T WANT THIS

Saw my old connect, rented me a spaceship. The town is very small, so, whatever is done on one side, trust me, it gets around fast. Rumors were spreading about the little episode. Pablo sent word, he wants the link chain back. He loaned it to Claudio.

My own so called Solido brother were mad that I got Pablo. Really, they just wanted to benefit from some of the dope.

Now that I robbed Pablo, he wasn't allowing his dope to be distributed on our side of town. Fine with me. This only made what I had like gold.

I got rid of my stuff fast. Every time I rode past Florence St. Kathy would try to flag me down. But I wouldn't pull over. I ignored her. Tables turned.

I guess she couldn't take it anymore. She saw me coming, and jumped in front of the car. I was either going to run her over, or stop for her. Of course I didn't run her over.

When I stopped, she opened the passenger side door and jumped in. I pulled to the curb, "what's good?" She stared me up and down, grinning hard, "look at you!" she kept saying that. Eye's fixed on the chain.

I was pissed at her still. She asked, "is this a rental?" "yeah, you need a ride somewhere?" She somehow got offended, "nah, I ain't getting out. I'm with you all day and night." One side of me, wanting to make the best of this situation and fuck her brains out, just to let her know. She could've been my wifey.

But the wiser side said, "hell nah." You didn't feel my style until the demon was out. "I didn't want this," but it was too easy to revert back to my old style. But I wasn't happy at all. Just had a few dollars. We smoked and went to KFC, the chick at the drive through was on me.

I had my gun and like $20,000 in my lap. She could see it all, birds eye view. She put her hand over the microphone and told me she was writing down her name, number and address.

Only thing she forgot was her social. Then she pretended like she had a phone to her ear and said "call me." Kathy snatched the phone number as soon as I put it down, then ripped it.

I thought that was hysterical. At the red light, these sisters tried to get my attention. I rolled down the window and asked, "what's good?" They wanted to know where the weed was.

I needed some myself, so I told them to follow me. At the spot it was like a fashion/car show. Few fake drug dealers showing off. Dudes got shook when I popped up.

The sisters who followed me, they peeped it. Dudes was pressing up on them, they told the dudes they were with me and cats started apologizing. I'm sorry miss, "Yo JB, I didn't know." The sisters were from New Britain.

Kathy was mad as hell. She said to me, "bitches act like they know you, they just met you at the light." She tried to kiss me on my lips, caught me off guard, but then I backed up.

Them New Britain girls really got a kick out of that. They probably thought she was my girl until they peeped that move. I took their number and made a date with them. "I'll come through New Britain in a few days. I'll call first, and the smoke is on me."

Gave both of them a hug and jetted with Kathy. She said, "you really feeling yourself huh?"

Now it's time to check this, "when I was broke and only trying to get to know you, you wanted no parts of me. Now, you're seeing the old me, I didn't want you to see this side, and now you with it."

She got really quiet, and so I didn't persist, we had a good day. I tried to drop her off a few times, she wouldn't get out of the car. So, I let her stay with me all night.

Went to the package store, got more weed, and went to the room. She tried repeatedly to initiate sed, but I kindly, softly as possible without injuring her feelings, declined. She saw my obvious excitement. I was hard as a rock, but, I didn't want to have her thinking we were together.

What I did with Dawn's little friend was out of control. What I did with Cookie's little friend was out of control. I can't keep doing this shit. Ill eventually kill someone over foolishness.

And this is not who I am. So, we laid there. I kissed her and rubbed her down. She liked it. Even moaned when I grabbed her ponytail and got a little rough with her.

I slept like a baby. On the drive to drop her off, I couldn't believe I didn't sleep with her. Before she got out, she kissed me. Real slow, and grabbed my joint. Then ran off like a little girl.

I thought before I drove off, What the fuck did last night mean? She's not my girl, and we aint on that wave.

As I was driving down Florence St. I saw Cookie and her moms standing in front of her house. Two children were playing in their yard. I wondered if they were Cookie's kids. Maybe, who knows.

I just realized I didn't have on the link chain. Kathy thinks this will bring me back over to her spot. She was wrong.

21 VOP How?

Usually in the underworld, when the criminal life is just coming together smoothly, something is about to happen. My money was good, violence in the hood was down considerably, block was booming. I'm like, wait a minute. Let me try something different here.

I stopped hustling cold turkey and got this pump my breaks job at stop and shop. It was in the deli department. I've never done anything like that before, but I proved to be a fast learner for things I attached passion to.

The job was only part time, but I stole every opportunity to work full time shifts. Everything was smooth, customers were feeling my style and I quickly got the rhythm.

I used to like giving the customers samples of the meat I was cutting for them. As much as they requested, fuck stop and shop Inc. I was for the people. It didn't matter their complexion. The customers, period, were my people. It was fun.

Often times, the female customers were sliding me numbers and invitations to the crib. I took a few up on their offers, but then they'd become my stalkers. I would catch chicks hiding in the store, pretending to shop. Just to spy on me, see if I was still taking applications.

They hired this new dude. His attitude was stank, I think he was like, Polish or something. We had the same job description, we were butchers.

I worked on one end of the department, and he on the other. I could be having a conversation with a customer and he would be staring all in my mouth.

We rarely spoke to each other, and that's the way I liked it. One of the female coworkers in the deli confided in me. She told me, the guy hates black people.

That automatically made me watch my footsteps around him.

One Sunday, on my day off. They called me in to work. I took the shift, despite having a strange feeling in my stomach that day. It was crazy cause my stomach didn't hurt until they asked me to come in. the pain came immediately, I ignored it. Bad move.

It was pretty busy in the deli, but this sucker was working. So all I wanted was the day to be over with. Right before my break, the dude and I were both needing some ham or something from the same display case.

I took the high road, let him go first. The customer didn't want his service though, she asked me to help her. That pissed him off, he said, "you want the Nigger?" I thought I was hearing wrong, had to be. Even the customer said something. Older white woman came to my defense and told him, "you should be fired for that comment," and walked away without getting her order.

I stepped to this young punk, I told him "if you ever talk to me or about me in that way, I'll cut your head off." I made sure to give this punk clear eye contact.

He was trembling. Then I went for my break. About 20 minutes into the break, my name is called over the store's intercom system. They never did that before, this was weird. I was summoned to the main office.

As soon as I walked in, I spotted 3 police officers, and the manager who never once spoke a word to me. He asked me if I threatened my coworker, and so, I was truthful. I told them, "he called me a Nigger," and the cops said, "well, aren't you?"

It took every ounce of restraint I never knew I possessed not to attack that fool and make him eat those words.

The cops and manager all laughed. I had no witnesses, and then, I was cuffed and walked out. Heated and embarrassed, they took me to their small town police station. This was an injustice. I'm in a cell, smelling like lunch meat, treated like dog shit. My bond was only $500, so I needed $50 to get out.

They barely gave me a call, but they had to, it was my right. I got out the next day at court. Since stop and shop was in East Hartford. I had to go to court in Manchester, which we called KlanChester.

They were known for being racist, their cops, their courts, KlanChester period. I felt it firsthand at the manager's office in stop and shop.

I felt crazy going to court for that BS.

The judge was talking to me like he really wanted me to do some jail time. That was crazy, but check this.

Some people standing on the side of the court Marshall's wanted to have a word with me, following these court proceedings. They were representing the office of adult probation.

They claimed, once upon a time, which I didn't recall. As part of my sentence, it was followed with3 years of probation. I was so called in violation of that 3 year probation. And they were there to inform me that they were seeking an arrest warrant on the charges of, "Violation of Probation".

They claimed not only did I fail to report, but also, getting this new threatening charge would've also been grounds for a violation warrant to be issued.

And so, I was arrested. Right then and there. The bond was set at $50,000. I wasn't getting out. Pissed wasn't a fit word.

So I went through another tour of incarceration.

I did the 3 years straight. No parole, no probation. No more rabbits in the hat.

I made sure this round.

My end of sentence date was in 2 days. August 15, 1999.

Hold on, shit is about to get interesting.

22 JACKY

August 15, 1999. A great day, bright, sunny with no chance of precipitation. I could've had someone pick me up from the jail, but instead, I set it up with the blocks counselor to get dropped off.

Gave my jail shit away, sneakers, cosmetics, extra sweatpants, t shirts, socks etc. For the cats less fortunate, mostly lifers.

The CO dropped me off in the state's suburban. It had a cage for the divider. Usually when prisoners are riding in it, they're rocking shackles, hands and feet. But since I was an official free man, the CO let me in without cuffs.

He dropped me off downtown Hartford, right at the front of the Civic Center. That's the spot where all the attractions are held. He had to open the door for me, they were locked from the inside.

I hopped out rocking grey sweats, a new t shirt, and shower shoes. A box with my property which consisted of photos of my family, a few letters, and a chess board which I brought home for nothing.

There were 3 ladies standing next to the suburban, it looked like they were on a lunch break. A white, black, and a Spanish one. They whistled at me as I walked away. I looked back, and these grown women were giggling like school girls.

As I approached the Civic Center's doors, some women were headed my way. So I paused, then opened the door for them all. One of the ladies touched my cheek and said, "so sweet."

But the pleasure was all mine. My appreciation for women was at an all time high. I've always been a gentleman. In my eyes, there's no other way to be.

I went to the pay phone, but I didn't have any money. So as this Latin sister passed, I stopped her and asked for 10 cents to use the pay phone. She looked me up and down, and said, "let me guess, you just got out?" But she already knew.

I flirted, "what gave me away"? Well, the shower shoes of course. And the phone costs 50 cents, not 10.

Wow, that fast. A lot of things had changed.

I called my sister. Nobody knew I was getting out. She came to get me, yeah, my little sister drives now. Even that was a sign of the times.

My moms no longer lived in the projects, she lived on the other side of town. A street called, Olds place. I didn't like it. The location was alright, but the house she rented was run down.

The landlord was a slumlord, for sure. And the worst part was, I knew him. Nasia was six now, her and Kamar. So Beautiful, both of them.

Dawn was married and pregnant, I actually was happy for her.

I went to Center St. to see if I could get some of the cats I knew to hit me with a few dollars. Dudes were out there rolling dice. "same old 2 step."

Jamal had the most money. Everybody was working for him. He knew me, he was scared to see me come up from scratch. Made excuses when I asked him for money. This would bite him one day, and he knew it. But what made him happy was that it wasn't today.

My projects, Bellevue Square, no longer stood the same. It was remixed. Well, it still was the square, but had different structure and different community rules, if you know what I mean.

"That old shit aint flying," basically.

My cousin Day Day still lived on Center St. His nephew Ty, who was my cousin also, was staying on Center at the moment. Ty introduced me to this cat named Cory. He was a good dude, went to college, worked, had a nice little car.

He basically became my Chauffeur. He didn't mind though, as long as I had weed. We hung out. Every now and then, I paid for gas.

I went to see Russian Vic, one of my old associates from the hood. His new spot was called New Jack. These old apartment buildings on Main St. All our old associates hung there.

Vic was a consistent dope dealer. He always had dope. Streets said he had fire. I asked him for 5 stacks, he gave it to me. "5 stacks" was $5000 worth of dope. He wanted back $2000. I sold it early morning on Center St. Gave Russian Vic his money back and didn't do it again.

I got a pound of AZ for $800, it was decent. It wasn't for sale.

I heard TJ Maxx had nice shit on the low, designer shit, so I went to check it out. I mostly bought under clothes. Chick doing the register was on me, and gave me her number.

But the one behind me, the customer, ran up on me when I left the store. Asked me to dead the register girl shit, and I wouldn't regret it. I gave her the math, she ripped it up. She flexed her new lacy thongs, pulled the out the bag. Teased me. Shits was like a magic wand. We went straight to her spot, the new condos next to Herbs and Sporting Goods.

I was in that building once before, my aunt lived there. Chick name was Janae. Cute dark skinned chick, 4 feet something. Usually not my type, but her aggression turned me on. That, and the fact that I didn't have sex in 3 years.

The condo was her moms, told me she was visiting from Miami. I believed her.

We smoked on the staircase. Then I smoked her in her empty room in front of the mirror. My pull ups, pushups, dip set, all that, I believe was incorporated in the sex. Super high voltage, high frequency, I did, what the weed couldn't do.

But she wasn't my chick. That came and went, literally.

Cory wanted me to take a ride with him to his school, CCSU, in New Britian, CT. He told some chicks he knew he would come to their dorm and smoke with them.

I was with it. As soon as I stepped in that building, I saw the most beautiful, perfect, woman of my dreams. She had to be, I never knew I had a dream girl, until I saw her. She wasn't revealing her body, or flexing. She just sat there, beautiful. Even now, it's hard to explain this beauty, but I felt mesmerized. Once we made eye contact, I knew it wasn't a fluke.

She had a Wu Tang Clan fitted on, some jeans, Nikes, a sweater, and eyes that pierced through my soul. This was crazy, even when we spoke to each other I felt magnetism.

Some dudes were crowded around her, whoever had her, had just lost her. Despite people talking all around us, we never broke eye contact. Eventually, cats recognized the obvious and peeled off.

I introduced myself, so did she, Jacky.

Jacky was my new favorite name in the world. She invited me to the bathroom, to get naked for her. I was ready, but she laughed and stopped me. Gave me her number, and told me to call her in a few hours.

This was my first time ever counting the minutes. Cory was pissed, he made plans for us to check those girls in her dorm. I was straight, all I could talk about after that was Jacky.

When I called her, she said come over. I still know that address. Park Avenue, East Hartford. I gave Cory 10 dime bags and gas money. I just needed to get there.

Talk about excitement. I ran up those stairs like Rocky. Walking into her apartment was like stepping into paradise. It was like, we were curious teenagers left alone.

We smoked. I'll never forget, she told me, "you aint getting no ___." I started laughing. She started laughing. We were on her couch.

Hands down, the sexiest chick I ever met. I took my clothes off, those little hands were all over me. She had this greedy, lusty look on her face. Every move she made, I was falling in love with her.

We went to her bedroom, then the shower. Some things she let me do in there, we going to act like that was Vegas and leave it there. Trust me, she's the best.

Without cheesy details, her love is the best I ever felt. While we were laying there, I told her, "I love you." I've never done that. Also, I never meant those words more.

She thought I was bugging, but I wasn't. If ever soulmates exist, she's that for me. I get turned on just looking at her. I don't mean naked, I'm talking driving from A to B, watching her brush her hair. Oh man, her hair, sexy, long, hypnotizing, spell binding, real, and smells so good! Nobody's fucking with Jacky.

I started looking for a job. Found one at this moving company in East Hartford. They told me straight out, no benefits, no medical, but I could make anywhere from $200-$400 daily if I put the work in. Oh and they pay daily or weekly, my choice. I chose daily, in cash.

I already had smoke and a few bucks left from that dope money, so the pressure wasn't too tight. I didn't want to just show up, and get my feelings hurt, so I called her. She let me come through.

I told her I found a job, and we both were happy about that. We celebrated with weed and sex. I felt like I knew her all my life. She was the perfect match for me.

Next day, she drove me to work. I'll never forget, as I was getting out of her car, I told her, "I loved her," she said, "she loved me too." Stopped me in my tracks, I rushed her, "what you say?"

From the look on her face, she hadn't planned that, but those words were said and my soul recorded them. And played them back, over and over again in my heart and mind. "Jacky loves me too."

At that moment, life felt so good!

Work was serious. I was one of two loaders on the truck and there was, of course, the driver. Which I learned that day, didn't have to help us load unless he chose to out of kindness, or maybe a big tip being involved.

The first job was in Avon, CT, this model's house. She was moving to a new spot and needed everything out. We started with the heavier things. Just made sense.

I was carrying her dryer down her spiral staircase and this chick wanted to come down the stairs alongside me. Watching my every move, yelling, "don't scratch the staircase." That shit was annoying.

Took about 5 hours to finish the whole spot. Then, we took it to the next spot and brought everything inside. This woman thought she hired interior decorators.

Altogether, that job itself was like 8-9 hours. We were off to the next one. We went to the attic, this sucker had a baby grand piano.

Good thing I was strong as an ox, because only us two cats did the lifting. Coming down the stairs was crucial. Another 5-6 hours, that job was finished. I was exhausted.

Like a 15 hour work day, the first day. Yikes.

We were headed back to the office, the driver had to drop the truck off there and secure the money in the office safe. The company made $1800, oh yea, I forgot to say that day we got $200 in tips each. Even the driver who didn't break a sweat.

I was pissed off. This was slavery. And the driver was acting like he was the boss of the operation and we were his workers. We stopped for gas, I asked the driver if he could drop me off when we got back to the office. Surprisingly, he said yes.

He dropped the truck off in the company's parking lot, and hid the keys. I guess that's standard routine, but the keys to the office weren't where they were supposed to be. So, he was bringing the money home and bringing it to work the next day.

He was dropping me off on the avenue. He ran into the bodega to get cigarettes, so I noticed the money. In a company pouch. I took out $1300 real quick. Left the rest of it.

We got to my stop. I thanked him and ran all the way to Day Days crib on Center St. Called up Cory, and went to the mall.

I spent that money in the Ralph Lauren shop. Nice slacks, nice socks. Nice button up, nice sweater vest. Nice polo boxers and a crisp pair of Wallabee Clarks; total, $800. And with the change, another $500 I had left. That remained in my pocket.

Went over to see Jacky, smoked and had fun. She couldn't believe I spent that amount on one outfit. Really, she knew at that time, I didn't have it like that.

I didn't tell her anything about what I did at work, or after work. I was embarrassed. And I needed her to respect me, because I was in love with her.

She ended up finding out anyway. She was the contact number at that job. They sent the cops to her crib, asked some questions about me, they really didn't know if I did it.

She told me about it afterwards. I was on Center playing C-Low, I was winning too, and this dude came through flexing. Only after he left, my Solido, so called brother, told me we just missed out on an opportunity of a lifetime.

"what's good," Hot Rod told me the dude just showed him 500 grams of heroin, but he's a brother. Meaning, he was Solid. I told Hot Rod, "fuck that, he's done. Where is he?"

The kid was from another town. I won't say, but he went to get weed on the Avenue before he got back on the highway, heading home. I figured he would pass by again before he left town. He had 2 chicks with him, and was showing off. Sure enough!

We were in the car with this sucker named Bump. He wanted a piece of the pie, so we followed the dude. He went to the south side to get Spanish food, but Hot Rod only had 1 gun and since they were close, he didn't want to be the one.

The dude knew Hot Rod really well, you could tell Rod was hesitant. He came out of the restaurant, tried to get in the whip. I rushed in, "yo, let me get that." It took maybe 10 seconds to realize that he was about to lose it all.

I got it, plus this chain he had, worth at least $30,000. Bump scary ass done drove off. So I turned to traffic. Opened the door of this Lexus, jumped in, aimed at the driver and told him, "get me out of here, North end. Let's Go!"

I made him run the red light, we was out. When we got somewhere else, we examined the heroin. It was real. This fool should've never came to Hartford to show off. Look what it cost him, could've been his life.

The guy who owned the Lexus was a damn drug dealer. Cat named Henny. For his cooperation and perfect timing, I let him have the chain. He couldn't stop thanking me.

Another reason I gave homeboy the chain, Rod wanted it for himself, but no way. So that settled it.

We got functioning addicts to cut the dope for us. "Who better than cats that got down?" It was fire, Mexican Mud, brown heroin.

Long story short, me and Rod had a falling out over splitting the work. I ended up with $20,000 worth out of $80,000 worth. I was tight, but I ate it.

Day Day's brother, Trevor, was my older cousin, he hustled but I knew he sniffed dope also. He heard about my fire, and wanted in. I gave him $5,000 worth, and told him to bring me back $1,500. Generous deal.

The first time went smooth, usually does. I hit him again. I. wasn't spying on him, but I overheard him say, he just ordered 9 ounces of crack and he was waiting for the dude right now.

What he ordered cost at least $4800 at the time, so I approached him, "I need my money." He went crazy. I was going to pop him, but his chick saved him. She came out of nowhere screaming.

Before I slid, I said, "when I come back, you better have me."

I smoked, then ate. Then I ate again, then smoked. Circling the north end, I tried to stay calm. But I wanted my money, so I went back to center. I didn't see Trevor, but I was looking.

I stopped at the stop sign, zoned out for a second. The cops rushed me., from all angles, 6 cruisers. Bumper to bumper, they boxed me in.

I jumped out, gun in my hand, pushed off the cruiser's bumper and ran as fast as I could. Threw the gun, just to get it out of my possession. So lucky they didn't blast me.

They got me. They always bring that dog out. I hate dogs.

23 JACKY'S MY BONNIE

I think she was offended, but told me straight up, no. she wasn't in a relationship and she was feeling me. That felt so good to hear. So we locked that in, Jacky was mine.

She started visiting me, she looked so good. I was so honored this beautiful woman was mine. She was super sexy, without trying.

At first, I had non contacts, so we had to talk on the phone behind bullet proof glass. It had its benefits, her freaky self used to show me her chest.

Day one I laid my eyes on her, she blew my mind. And every visit, she kept doing that.

We had good communication, I loved talking to her. She drove me crazy.

I asked her over and over was she really going to wait for me. She assured me she would.

I believed her, but it wasn't easy. She's so beautiful.

After a few months, I got my contact visits back. The first one we had, blew me away. When she walked in, looking so good, I wanted to yell to the moon, "My chick is BAAAD!" I'm serious.

I felt like, everybody wanted to be me, the other prisoners of course, but even the correctional officers. And other free people on that visiting room floor.

I'll love her for the rest of my life. Easily. She's my baby. Few times she brought me smoke. But that wasn't the best part of her visiting. The best part was, my lips on her lips, my arms around her, her eyes, staring into my eyes. And me knowing that, this beauty is mine.

I know she "did her", while I was in, but she's the love of my life.

Time flew, before I knew it I was arranging for her to come pick me up.

That was a great day. She came to get me from Carl Robinson prison at 9am. Soon as out bodies met, she jumped on me, wrapped her legs all the way around me.

She gave me a rose. That was a first for me.

We drove off, I felt numb, her little freaky ghetto self. She had a piece rolled up, ready for me. I lit it, took me some deep totes, got a buzz instantly.

She kept staring, and sailing. I bet I could've read her mind. She brought me to see my family for a few hours, while she handled some of her business. Then she came for me, brought me home.

She moved to a different spot, still in East Hartford though. We lived in Mayberry Village, some people would say it was a project, but to me, it wasn't. More like town houses.

Upstairs, downstairs, 1 ½ bathrooms, 2 bedrooms. It was nice. We sat on that famous couch and smoked. She had the nerve to say to me, "we don't have to fuck until you're ready."

Yea right, lets go! We went upstairs, had fun. My voltage was high, only 2 years away, but I still needed readjustment.

I would meet her son, James, on a very different note as before. He was 5 last time, now he's 7. He hadn't come home from school yet.

I lived with Jacky this time, things were different.

I even got to know her moms better. I had to, Jacky was officially part of my life.

Thank god, me and James got cool. I started bringing him to school when she left for work. It felt good. Slowing down a bit, doing regular human being stuff.

James actually liked me walking him to school. I did too. I met his teacher all that. When he came home from school I was right there waiting.

I really loved when my baby came home from work. I would be waiting at the door like a puppy waiting to get fed, but I wasn't waiting for food. I was waiting for a__.

Jacky's. those kisses as soon as she came in, was juicy. Me and James would be waiting for them shits.

James used to say to me, "J.B. you love mami don't you?" And Id say, "yes, James. I love your mami. Shes my mami too." And he would laugh. I would too.

My life, my soul needed Jacky and James in them.

Jacky wanted me to stay broke and humble, and safe at home with her and James. Although I was enjoying being home with them, I needed to contribute financially.

A man has to, really. I wouldn't feel totally comfortable until I paid all the bills. But for now, I have to at least bring money to the table. My baby didn't pressure me at all, but I felt crazy being broke. I did something.

Cory was still on deck. I needed his service. I contacted my little brother Nate, He had kids now and all that, and an apartment in our old project. But remixed now, it was called Mary Shepard's place.

Named after Mrs. Mary Shepard, from our project. She lived there, it was said, at least 60 years. She was over a hundred years young. She's still alive god willing

Nate was still hustling, but nothing major. Be he held his house down like a man was supposed to, even lived in the same crib with his baby moms and kids. I respected him for that.

Where we from, you rarely see that anymore. Pop's is out, after he gets his shit off.

I couldn't talk. At that point, I was also one of the terrible ones. God willing, one day I'll fix that.

I had a weird plan. It was unique. I wanted, Nate, My cousin Day Day and myself to make an album, well CD now, in the studio with all the hot beats out people like.

Make tens of thousands of copies, and sell them, hand to hand in Virginia. I just had this feeling we could do it, and find many new opportunities.

They were down. We happened to find this studio, not far at all, from our stumping grounds.

Jamaican dude named I Feel, owned the studio in the same building as this hair salon.

Now, all we needed was some money to pay for the studio time and a few other things in preparation of our trip to V.A.

Jacky was opposed to the idea, me leaving to another state, being away from her and James. Plus she knew, I was known to get out of control. To say the least.

I had Cory drive me and Nate around town. Hood to hood basically, smoking and brainstorming. Look who I see posted up like he had license to slang shit in the hood? Hotty!

I made Cory park, but we didn't get out. Cory had nice little tints, we were invisible.

Hotty definitely was pushing dope. Nate still had a few dollars, he was actively selling dope. So this was right up his alley. Peep the fly shit.

I had Nate purchase an ounce from Hotty. People went crazy for his stuff. China White, so I hear, and the quality was high.

So while Nate was making good profits, and satisfying his custeez, Hotty was trusting him, falling right into the trap. We went ahead and booked some studio time for next week.

Every move calculated, even the making of the music. We would, make our CD, test the product on the public, see if the streets would hop on it.

Then plan our trip out of state, depending on the response.

A great day to get busy. On all levels, it was the 3rd of the month. I had Nate go ahead of me, and order 4 ounces of heroin from Hotty. Hotty told him, meet him at the spot.

Little did he know, we already there. A few cats I knew, medium league hustlers were purchasing from Hotty. Real quick, in and out, pretty slick operation.

While him and Nate were in the hallway doing business, I popped up.

Hotty looked like he saw a ghost. I grabbed him by the shirt, my gun out, he knew what it was. He gave up the diesel, but when I went for the money, he tried to play tough.

His girl was right in front of the building with a little girl. Maybe his daughter. His chick saw what it was, raw in the middle of the street screaming, "they robbing my man."

No time to be tussling with this fool, he tried to run, I tried to get his head, "blah blah." I missed. It's a good thing.

Me and Nate, hopped a fence, then got under the tints. Cory was shook, until I told him, "you aint do nothing" calm down and drive regular."

Straight to the studio, called up Day Day. He met us there, perfect timing.

Sent Cory to buy some weed for us, and some dutches.

Get twisted, then hop in the booth. That was the plan.

I splattered this Mobb beat, this was the part about being around us lions, that Cory loved witnessing.

Ping ponging the blueberry, flow on a different frequency/
next level adrenaline, make y'all seem measly/
Hard to survive in these killing fields we made seem easily/
Way liver than Cinemax, just pop in the DVD/
I'm Hasan, earths oldest six grader/
Let me take you to age 11 dog, a born regulator, my mama name's Adrienne, had a few cesareans, 12/2/73. I'm a Sagittarius.

Since a youth, took a liking to coupes/
Ma dukes sat our ass down, made us watch the roots/
Thoughts appeared in my mind, I'll never get out/
Like fiends, shooting in they dick, while they foam out the mouth.

Dreads moved in our building, my first QP/
Said bring back 250 and the rest "do me"/
In elementary was popular, had all the chicks/
Big bags of now and laters and chico stix/

Building 21 K, lived on the 4th floor/
Still went to school fresh, but we was dirt poor/

First trip to Broad St, that's juvenile holmes/
Wooden bench in a cell damn, I wanna go home/
Cant cry for mommy, she aint gon hear it/
Lost both her jobs coming to my court hearings/

Judge threw me probation, after hitting a sec/
Violated that shit fast, already I'm back/

Returned to the strip, burner on my hip/
Say you get what you give, well, lets see what I get/

24 VA

We did 8 altogether, 2 songs I did dolo. Nate did 1 dolo and the others we blended combinations. The sound engineer and Cory were out judges. They gave us 2 thumbs up.

I met this polish woman, older lady who used to work for a big music group. She quit, and started doing her own business in her house.

She burned us 3000 copies of our CD for $2000. That was a good deal. We were slanging them in the streets of Hartford for $10 a pop.

Most of the sales came from the South End. My Latin people showed support crazy. The north end cats, I expected to hate, and they did.

We made a thousand dollars back, fast. That was a good sign, my plan wasn't to be in small town Hartford with them. The plan is Virginia, but, I wanted Nate and Day Day to see my vision. So that was a field test.

Day Day or Cory wasn't coming to VA with us. Just Nate and myself. That was cool, we gave Day Day 200 CD's for himself. He could make $2000 from that, if he was confident in his product.

When Jacky saw that I wasn't playing about the VA move, she was tight. I understood where she was coming from. I mean, it was risky, and the vision took balls. It was out there. Selling my own CD in another state, hand to hand like its crack to get on my feet. "Yeah, I'm wilding."

But that's how much confidence I had.

Now here I go, my high risk, always pushing it to the limit ass. I was thinking, "yea CD's is the main focus, but why not bring some crack out there also. Just to test the waters."

This cat I was alright with just got killed on Main st. Right by the hood, over winning a chess game. They were having a candlelight vigil in Sands. The next project over from mine.

I knew this cat named Richie, he sold crack, no nickels and dimes. He was medium level at least.

I got his beeper number from somebody. He knew who I was, so, I was shocked he was willing to serve me.

The meet was set up. He was at the candlelight vigil, maybe he was thinking this was a safe setting with all the witnesses and such. "I don't know."

Nate and I appeared, with no intention to pay, let me add.

We exchanged words briefly. I wanted to see the stuff. He brought something, but it was way less than what I requested. I wanted 4 ounces, he brought 2.

I straight, we were taking them anyway. Literally, we came for the, "free .99 special."

He was foolish enough to put them in my hands. Nate and I looked at each other. Smiled, then started walking away. Richie and his host were walking up on us, Nate and I had kitchen knives. No guns for this event.

Richie got aggressive, he ended up on the ground with a serious wound to the abdomen. Somebody poked him. He almost died, but he survived.

Nate and I ran back to his spot in the square.

This wasn't the plan, but sometimes you have to improvise.

Eventually, cops were on the scene. Ambulance all that. We got away, but the part I felt bad about is, my baby Jacky came to pick me up and she went over to the vigil spot, where the mess was made.

So when she asked dudes have they seen me, they got angry and maybe said some threating words to my love.

It may have frightened her a bit. She didn't deserve that. That was all my fault, and only reason I didn't come back for another date, and make them eat their words, was because I didn't want to oppress the land.

She picked me up at the super 8 hotel, she cursed me out. We went home, had fun still, and smoked before we slept it off.

All packed up, huge, duffle bags full of CD's, few ounces of crack, a few dollars, nothing serious. We were broke. Jacky dropped us off at the bus station and waited with us until the bus for VA came.

I kissed her sweet lips, and headed out on my mission. I can't imagine what was going through her mind when I got on that bus.

After stopping and switching busses in New York, altogether, it took like 12 hours.

We got off that bus like we stepped on another planet. I have 3 brothers on my father's side, Kareem, Raheem, and Antwoine, they lived in VA.

I was the oldest of all my father's kids. Kareem was next in line. I called Kareem up, I let him know beforehand, I was coming out there to hustle. He was expecting me.

I don't think he knew, I would only need his spot to hold down my CD inventory. Him and his chick Stacy had a town house.

Stacy was originally from DC, she had my brother Kareem twisted. Well, whipped is the right word. Kareem worked as an engineer on a railroad yard. He had a career.

So while Kareem was at work, Stacy just did whatever until he came home. They smoked weed heavy, like Nate and I did. And Kareem used to rap too.

First night there, we smoked, and had a little cipher. Kareem had some instrumental beats, it was fun.

But the next day when Stacy dropped him off for work, she drove us around to different parts of the town. We hopped out in every hood and sold CD's.

We did this all the way to my brother's lunch break. It was a good first day. We treated Stacy to lunch, for taking us all around town.

Quickly we knew what spots were more lucrative that others for our mission. Stacy was fascinated how Nate and I just started doing what we set out to do, with no delays.

His reward for driving us around was, gas money of course, free weed to smoke, and free lunch. Her life must have been super boring before our arrival, you could tell, she was excited just watching us hustle.

In less than a week we had $2,000. We met Kareem's cousin Smitty. All he did was work and be whipped also by his chick. He worked hard every day, then came home and babysat hit chick's son.

Cute little kid but wasn't his. On top of that, she was a bird, and didn't even work. So far these dudes are unbelievable, suckers.

Smitty had good credit, I gave him $500 to rent us a car for the week, he did it, plus kept the change. We didn't care about that though. We no longer needed Stacy.

We didn't stay at my brother's crib anymore. We got hotels. We stayed at this ran down joint called, The Travelers Inn. One of the projects was right across the street from the Inn. We were still selling CD's, but quickly recognized other opportunities in the town.

We were in Portsmouth. They had maybe 4 projects, and we got familiar with them all. At this joint called Howard Holmes Project, we met this kid there, he sold us some weed. We smoked up all our good stuff and now we had to deal with their garbage.

While at the dudes crib, I noticed his scars. Asked him what he was hit with, he said a S.K. Until then, we never knew what a SK was, everybody's heard of an A.K, A.R 15 etc.

Nate wanted one of them. He became a fan. Homeboy told us he could get guns cheap. We couldn't believe the prices he mentioned. After we made a few more thousands we'd see if he was bluffing or not.

What we were accustomed to selling for 20, they sold for 100. We quickly did the math. These two little ounces were worth more than what we expected.

It was a Friday night, we still had 5 more days with the car we rented. The projects ran dry. No one had crack. So we sat in this crack house and allowed the owner of the crib to serve all his guests.

Everything went in 3 hours and we made $5,000. So we planned on going back to Hartford, getting triple what we had, and seeing how that would go.

But the plot thickens, we bought too many guns for only $4000. We had duffle bags full, all kinds. So we would risk the trip to and from, all or nothing. Lets go!

Nate drove, while I planned our every move on out. It was exciting and risky as hell. One false move, and we were down for the count.

First trip went smooth. It took 7 ½ hours to get back around the way. Great timing. We both checked in with our women. Jacky was home, where I wanted her to be. I surprised her, she didn't know I was coming back. Well not that soon anyway.

We had fun, smoked, and had more fun. Then, I left to pick Nate up. We still had to get rid of the guns and get some crack before we got back on the highway and headed back to the spot.

Spanish dudes on the south end bought every last burner. Asked for more, I told him I would be back.

So the $4,000 worth of guns we brought, turned to $15,000. This was definite progress.

Before we hopped back on that highway we checked our girls again real quick. Jacky didn't want me to go, but I told her. "I'll be back. I'm making progress. I love you."

And it was true, all of it. We stopped in the City (New York) to get some crack and some good weed for us, the weed in VA was terrible. My Dominican people gave us 9 ounces for $4500. We wanted more, but we had to see how this would go down first.

25 ALL OR NOTHING

We did a lot in 24 hours.

The spot in VA was still a gold mine. No one in that side of town had crack. We reopened shop at the crack house. Word got around fast.

Traffic didn't stop until it was all gone. It was crazy. Felt like we had earth to ourselves. Not a cop in sight.

Nate and I fell back. Let the house man run his house. He smoked crack for free and put a couple of dollars in his pocket at the same time. He was a happy camper.

By Monday, early Monday morning, it was all gone. We broke that work down, dime for dime. You wouldn't believe it.

That $4,500 investment turned into $27,000. Not to mention we still had thousands left from the gun sales.

We still had like 2 days left on the rental, so we went to see my brother Kareem. His mind was blown. He heard a little something about our adventures. He couldn't believe it.

Until I had him call his cousin Smitty back up. Smitty came to meet us at Kareem's. We smoked that good stuff, and jetted back to the rent a car spot. Time to re-mix the whip. Even though we still had 2 days credit. Kareem and Stacy watched Nate hand Smitty the $500 for the next car like it was gas money. I counted out $30,000 in front of them. Their mouths were open the whole time.

We upgraded the car, we had it for 7 days. We spent the 2 days we had left on the upgrade. It was a good move. More space to move, more luxury. Smitty took his little fees and was good. As a bonus, for his assistance, we hit him with a couple dimes of that good, and copped more guns from that dude. This time, he introduced us to a bigger connection. This white dude had his own gun shop and was ex military.

The big difference about doing business with him was, all the guns were brand new. I could most likely ask for more.

The risk was increasing every trip. We spent $20,000 on weapons. I didn't even make an estimate of what our profit might be, but I knew it was a nice piece.

We headed on our journey. It was surely dangerous.

We stopped in New York briefly. I wanted to get Jacky some Clothes and Bags. Nate and I picked out some things for our kids and ourselves as well.

Got back to Connecticut, checked in with our women, I surprised my baby again. Had fun with her, smoked, and watched her get excited over the things I grabbed for her.

What I loved so much about her was, she sincerely loves me. She really didn't care about me hustling and taking these risks. Let me say this the right way. She didn't want me husting and taking the risk of going back to jail.

She wanted me for me. Nothing material. Her love was so beautiful to me and I neglected it by continuing to take the risks that I did.

Once again, went out to get the guns off. Same cat from the south end copped them. And for that reason, I didn't raise the price.

It was safe to deal with one person. And we basically were already locked in with each other after the first deal.

He gave up $42,000. This was crazy. $22,000 profit, plus we still had a few loose thousands. We split the money 50/50.

Now we called up Cory. Got him to rent us a car, and we still had the other one from VA.

Time was of the essence, had to hurry up back to VA, take advantage of the drought. Had fun with my baby, then hopped back on that highway.

We stopped In the city again. We couldn't find the connect and was forced to deal with someone new. That was scary. Few blocks up, this kid called himself Bin Laden, should've known better. But I tried him out. Well, a fool I was.

It took like an hour to finally get something from him and boy, was it a mistake.

Since we were kicking it, I rolled the dice. Got the whole thing. 36 ounces. A kilo, it looked good, fish scale, but looks can often be deceiving and they were in this case.

It was powder, we spent $18,000 on it. Well, I spent 18 on it. I owned my mistake.

Gor some more weed for the trip, and more, and headed out. We got there 7 hours later. Straight to the crack spot. The house man said he knew how to cook the coke up, so we let him, but not all of it at once just in case he didn't really know his shit.

He kicked everybody out while he had this operation going on. It took a while, he did it in the microwave like someone else I once knew.

We lost out, but still wasn't losing it all. He cooked up 9 ounces, a fourth of the work. It only came back to 6 ounces, lost 3 ounces on that round.

Not the worst. The quality of what we did have was good, but what happened was, the dudes must have cut it up with some garbage trying to stretch what they had. This happens a lot.

We sold out in 2 days and made $13,000 off that. We still had 27 ounces left, but I tried something different. I heard around the town that powder was in demand.

This would make up for a lot of loss. People that sniffed it, didn't require the same quality as someone who would cook it up.

We went to a few different spots in Portsmouth. Found some candidates in a project called KP. We sold the ounces whole for 2,000. It was still profit. Sold 15 to 3 different dudes, had 12 left.

We put this cat on, we met him at the bodega. I overheard him speaking with someone, his spot was booming, but nobody had work in his hood. For a month.

I was thinking, shit, they would take whatever they could get their hands on, and they did. Took longer than we wanted, but he moved 6 ounces in one day.

Gave it to him on credit, for $2,000. He still made $13,000 for himself, don't ask me how, because I couldn't tell you myself, but he did it.

So we came with the last 6 for him. Nate went into his house to get the dude, but he took a while to answer the door. Finally he did. I watched Nate go in.

Out of nowhere, detectives rushed in, boxed the rental in on all sides.

Brought back a bad memory, damn.

When Nate came out of the house, they snatched him up too. The coke was stashed in the rental car, they found it. Charged us, brought us to the precinct, but not the dude we were bringing it to. I'm thinking, this sucker set us up.

At the precinct, the cops separated Nate and me. The car was parked, and no one was driving it, nor sitting in the driver's seat.

I told the cops, "we don't have drivers licenses, how could we be driving that car?" The keys were already in the ignition dangling.

Maybe someone else is driving, but not us. They were pissed, thought we were wasting their time.

They charged us with operating a drug factory, and interstate trafficking. Big charges, and we were out of state.

We didn't get a bond, just a cell. No phone calls, but they did take our nice clothes and give us a little red identification bracelet. And jumpsuits.

"Clank, clank," the door slammed.

26 CAREFUL WHAT YOU WISH FOR

In order for Nate and I not to be in separate parts of the jail, we had to get put in the hole. Small death row cells. We agreed. We needed to strategize and stick together. If not, that commonwealth state, would've smoked us.

They let us have a chess board in the cell, Nate played good. He won all the games, I was pissed. I always hate to lose. They were so sick in that jail, knowing we had rights to make a phone call, they let us attempt, but at 3am when regular tax paying citizens are fast asleep.

At first, we had no bonds, seemed like we were kidnapped, but then we got one. Good thing we had money stashed at Kareem's house. Even he didn't know. We stashed it in our duffle bags of CD's. Perfect, I thought, who would've known?

We gave Kareem the instructions, and he came to get us, but before this was at all possible, I made a deal with God. I asked him, if he got Nate and I out of this situation and back to Connecticut safely, "If I screwed up again, let me be in prison for over 10 years."

I put sincerity, along with tears on that vow to god, and by his mercy, he came through for us. I recognize that now. Stepping out of jail, out of that cell, was like being reborn. Kareem got me out first. Don't forget we had 2 rented cars at one time.

The cops had the one with VA plates, but not the one with the CT plates.

We had it parked by Kareem's crib. I went straight to it, we had the other half of the money stashed there.

I had Kareem go pick Stacy up, asked her to drive me around to handle something real quick, and then go get Nate out.

I made Stacy bring me to see the gun connect. After bonding out, we still had $16,000 left. I spent $10,000 on more weapons.

We made it back to Kareem's to think it out. Nate was already there. We had our smoke stash also in the second car, so we wouldn't smoke it all up fast.

Now, we needed it. We all smoked and talked. Kareem thought I was a madman. We gave him $3,000 for his troubles, he was good. Then packed for our getaway trip.

The bondsman, told us clearly, "don't leave the state until we made all of our court appearances." But we wasn't trying to hear that shit. We were out that night.

It felt crazy jumping on that highway. It was all or nothing for real, for real.

We still had a few thousands left when we made it out of VA. We stopped at one of the rest stops, gassed up, ate some food and smoked.

That's when I pulled the duffle bags out of the trunk and put them into the backseat. Nate was shocked out of his mind.

He didn't know I made that last move with our money, but, we didn't come out to VA to lose money. We came to get money. So we were leaving with at least, some sort of money.

I was exhausted, all that strategizing and stressing, and thinking about Jacky.

Nate woke me up in a panic. We were getting pulled over. Life was over for us. I asked him, what happened, he said he was flying. Doing like 90 miles an hour.

Had to think fast, hold up.

I told Nate, first, pull over, he did. Before the state trooper got out of his car, I made the plan. "Yo, im gonna try to talk to him down. See if he let us go, if not, I got my chrome 45 under my thigh. I told Nate to have his 40 cal glock ready. He was a lefty, so he had it right in his hand, leaning in the pocket of the drivers side door.

I told Nate, "If he don't let us rock, I'm popping his wig. After I do, if you don't hit him too, I'm hitting you next."

Nate had an unexplainable look on his face. The state trooper was walking up on the car. First thing he said, "license and registration please?" My heart racing.

I started reasoning, "yo state trooper," and looked at his name tag, "Frasier. I know my brother was driving fast, please man give us a break. If you take us down, it would ruin our progress in life.

We selling CD's out the trunk, we started from scratch. Please let us rock"

The state trooper looked at us, and said, "you don't have a license, you were speeding. You could have a body in the trunk for all I know. But some reason, God is telling me to give you brothers a break.

Don't ever forget State Trooper Frasier if you make it in the music business." God is great.

Even though I wasn't what you would call a religious person, I still recognized that god was sparing me. Over and over again. He really was, no question about it.

As we drove off, Nate and I were just too shocked to speak for a second. Then I sparked up another piece and got twisted.

State trooper Frasier was black, had he not been, our goose was cooked. God sent the right one.

We stopped in the city once again. Got our kids some clothes, and got Jacky a few things, oh and some weed of course.

We made it back, nice and smooth. This time, instead of going home first, we got rid of the guns AYAP.

Sold them for $22,000. Not bad at all. Spent 10, made $12,000 profit. We split it 50/50. Called Cory up, remixed the rental, got another one. Fresh week start.

Jacky jumped on me, flooded me with love. I told her, fuck VA, it was music to her ears.

Later that day Nate and I found this Buick Regal on sale on Main St. $4,500. We got it, insured it, and registered it fast. It was white, no dents, and rode smooth.

We switched all the time. Sometimes I took the regal, he get the rental, and vice versa. We made it work.

After a few weeks, money was getting low. Bondsman from VA was hitting Nate's phone, asking him if we were going to show up for court. He told them, "yea, we will be there, 9am sharp." Yeah right.

After being in that town, like the one in VA having all the drug sales in the hood to myself, I didn't feel right scrambling in these CT streets again. That was out.

So we needed a new way to get it in.

Banks would be that new way. One early morning, we parked the rental a few blocks away, hopped in this bucket we got briefly from an addict, ran inside the bank. Had our faces covered up with hoodies. I jumped over the counter, ate 3 drawers, jumped back over and we fled. Nice and calm.

That took about 45 seconds. If we kept that timing, we would always be unstoppable. Timing was everything.

While in the bank, I saw blank money orders in the drawers, so out of curiosity, I grabbed a stack. We'd figure out what could be done with them later.

We drove the bucket to where the rental was parked, hopped in the rental, and went about our lives. It was $18,000 in cash. Not bad for 45 seconds. We found our new hustle.

I knew somebody, that knew somebody who worked in a bank. I gave this person some of the blank money orders, to see if they were valid or not.

Turns out, they were not. But the third party who worked in a bank, turns out, didn't work in a bank. In fact, she worked at a credit union.

She was saying how, sometimes her and her colleagues would be counting $700,000, before placing it in the safe. This would be every Friday. But they also leep $100,000 or better on any given day of the week.

Now at length, I thought about my old celly, Kev, from DC. He went to the feds for robbing credit unions. He showed me his numbers, big numbers. His paperwork was impressive, "I must do my homework."

I sent Nate to peep the scenery, go inside the place, let me know what it looks like. See if they had a security guard, and if so, is he armed?

Also, when he left the spot, to pay attention, how far away should we park the second car?

That was the homework, and it was enough info for me to prepare to go in. Only one thing, I had to find recruits for this job, to go in with me.

Since Nate rolled with me hard body through all my crazy adventures, and didn't change on me, I vowed that whatever money I made on my missions, he would eat too.

My sister's boyfriend Quan was a good dude, went to church, had a good character, wasn't wide open in the streets. I liked him.

He told me his brother was out of control, shooting people, getting shot, all that. So, I met him, basically gave him an interview, minus the application. I hired him and hoped I wouldn't regret it. I was told the biggest lump sum in the credit union was held on Friday. But the homework was done Tuesday, Wednesday we in there. I can't wait until Friday.

27 THE CREDIT UNIONS

I made Quan and his brother hang out with me all night, being that they knew my plans for tomorrow. We smoked weed and watched movies in the car all night parked on a side street.

I told Jacky I wouldn't be home until tomorrow, don't think I'm out here cheating. I was on a mission, wish me safety. She always did, I love her so much.

Showtime would be at 9:15 AM exactly.

Nate would be in the clean car waiting for us, and we would leave the dirty car parked somewhere.

"It's go time," Nate was in place. He didn't have to be there, but, he chose to.

As we pulled up in the spot, the brothers were scared to death. They tried to back out, but I built their confidence, we were good. I parked the dirty car in a way where when we came out, we could just go. No backing anything up, no obstacles, smooth sailing.

I ran in first, these cats were right behind me. I jumped straight over the counter. Made the women back away from the foot, silent alarm, "yeah, I know about that."

I asked the woman standing closest to me, where was the safe? She pointed to it, it was already ajar. I grabbed all the money stacks and went straight to the drawers.

Jumped back over again, and walked out with my crew. Nice and easy. I left the car running. We made it to where the clean car was, hopped in with Nate, blended in with the morning commute.

Went to Nate's crib, no one was there. I made everyone fall back while I counted the loot. We were all in the same room, but I clearly controlled the lane.

I told Nate, take the bullets out the other cats guns. I wasn't worried or anything, but sometimes, I would even get sick thoughts. After all, we are humans.

Nate did it, then stood right beside me. Soon as I counted past $100,000, I slid it under the bed. There was still a nice piece left to count afterwards.

When I put the 100k under the bed, me and Nate looked right at each other, like, exactly, they didn't need to see that. For what.

The rest was $75,000, so $175,000 altogether. Not good work, great work. In one minute flat, can't beat it. Paid better than a doctor, look Ma, I'm successful.

I gave the brothers $15,000 each for their cut. Then kindly asked them to take off. Didn't let them call a cab, no nothing. They walked away with $15,000, they got picked up the night before with empty pockets. How could they complain.

I gave Nate $40,000 on the strength he was my little brother. I had $105,000 to the face. I sat back and relaxed, while Nate went to get us some smoke.

I wanted to be home. Jacky didn't go to work, and I know she was worried about me crazy.

The drive back home was very different. How? I had $105,000 in fresh bills in a brown paper bag, sitting in the passenger side. And, I need not get pulled over, or harassed by anyone or thing in any way.

"Yes!" made it home. Jacky was laying on the bed, looking like the baddest chick I ever saw in my life. And, it wasn't the clothes, it wasn't nakedness, it wasn't words, but what it was—was pure genuine love for me. This woman is perfect for my soul. I'm telling you she didn't care about the money. God gave her to me.

I put the money at the top of the stairs, walked in the bedroom, squeezed and kissed my baby up passionately. Then faked like nothing went down.

I walked to our bathroom, which was next to out bedroom. Then told her, "grab that bag, Ma. Count it up and tell me what you think."

I was trying to roll up a piece without laughing. She was making, cute lady sounds. Excited, "I'll never forget it." She said, 'baby, do you have to give anybody any money?" I said "nah mami, that's all us."

We smoked then had fun like always. Maybe an hour later, Nate called me, said he just bought a tough max.

Jacky talked to me about how I'm always renting cars and didn't have one of my own, which she was right.

So we fixed that. We went to a few car dealerships, everything was garbage. Then we passed by this joint on Tower Ave. I saw this truck, a black Yukon, looking lonely. So I rescued her.

Me and my baby adopted her. Paid in full on the spot. Went to pick Nasia up. Paid the insurance that day. Picked James up from school, now I had my daughter, my stepson, and my baby on deck with me. We went to put some rims on the truck. I let the kids pick out the rims. James did actually.

He liked that, paid for them while they were putting them on the truck. We stepped outside, all of us, there was a car dealership next door to Tires Plus Wheels. I saw a black Bonneville. Nice low miles. They wanted $10,000, got it. Now we hopped in the rental, went back to the insurance place, added this one also to our new policy.

Paid full coverage, for a year, up front, then went back to get the truck. It was almost ready. But now, we needed to pick out rims for the Bonny, we brought her next door too.

Now both the joints were done up. Black and chrome. The truck had 20 inch rims and the Bonny had 18 inch rims. Clean, no payments, insured. Ready to go.

But we needed someone to drive the rental away. We got it done, it was a great day.

2 out of 3 of my kids, and Jacky. Definitely one of my favorite days.

28 TURNED UP

Jacky and I were feeling good about life. We were healthy and happy. Also trying to get pregnant. Started having a basic life routine, shed go to work, like always, and I'd drop James off for school. Then patrol the streets.

Nasia's and Kamar's birthdays were coming up so I got their sizes, went shopping in New York for them. Took Nate with me. It felt good.

I delivered Nasia's stuff first. She lived in Bloomfield. Dawn and her husband were doing great. Had a real impressive house. 2 cars in their driveway, and a huge backyard. I was really happy for her. She deserved to be happy.

I rang the doorbell. Dawn came out, we talked real quick before she got my baby. She was just making sure I didn't get my daughter's hopes up high, only to break her heart. Dawn knew me, and she knew I couldn't stay out of trouble at all. She was right.

My baby was happy to see me. I hugged her, kissed her, wanted to take her with me, Dawn wasn't having that. I took her gifts out of the truck, nothing was wrapped up. This was my baby, and she didn't need babying. She was very advanced for her age.

Before I left, I kissed her, and gave her a few dollars. Nate was there, he gave her a few dollars also. Made her smile. Dawn's sister in law came out to see what was good, she told Dawn, "you left that man, for my brother, you're crazy. Hook me up!" Dawn frowned. I smiled hard as hell.

Next stop, my son Kamar's house. I finally found out where he lived. Kim, his moms was alright with me coming over to see him anytime I wanted. I would smoke weed with her while I was there, but I never pressed up for sex. She had her life, and I had mine. Plus, I tried to hook Cory up with her.

I asked my son, "what do you want me to get you, specifically, that you've always wanted?" He said, "A lot of clothes, some timberland boots, and most of all for me to spend time with him." That last request broke my heart in pieces. Wow.

This beautiful son of mine.

Before I left that night, I gave him $300. His little eyes got big. That was funny.

After that night, I would pop up often. I went to Kim and asked her, if I could get my son? Let him stay with me and my girl, and James. She wasn't having it, but I was serious. I told her and Dawn, that I needed that. My kids would force me to do things differently in my life. The answers from both of them, was an unsurprising, "hell nah."

I loved picking James up from school, and so did he. He would have his little mans and them jump in the truck, and he liked when I had the music banging, loud as hell, he was the coolest kid in the school. And I dressed him, he was fly.

The crib was only a few blocks away, but the drive there was fun. I loved that James called me Daddy, he was my son too. And I loved him.

Every not and then I would help him with his homework. Picture that, a sixth grader, helping a first grader.

Nate and Quan was taking a trip to New York, they were driving Nate's Maxima up there, they had these chicken heads rolling with them. I had a bad feeling soon as I saw the cheap chicks. Pardon me.

My feelings were right, the next day I found out, one of the girls that went to the city with them, Nate took back to the hotel with him. I always got hotels with cameras and security settings, except for the time we stayed at the Travelers Inn.

But we got wise since and upgraded. Nate slipped up, and got a room in the hood, and paid the penalty.

It seems, Nate let them women see his money. He bought lots of clothes for himself and his kids, some pounds of weed, and let one of them stay the night with him. Big mistake.

She called her boyfriend up, while he was asleep. Told the dude to bring gun and a friend, they robbed Nate and almost beat him to death. They even stripped him naked and took his Maxima.

I found this out, I was furious. Nobody does this to my people and get away with it. Nate had staples all in his head. He was hurt bac, but he was strong.

I had my baby rent him a car. A fast Chevy Impala, new joint.

I parked the truck, called up Cory, because he had a license and got loaded up with clips and guns. We went on the hunt. Nate remembered where the chick lived, so we went there first. Had Cory park up the street, just in case. We didn't want him witnessing what we did. He was innocent.

The window was cracked open, no one was in the house. Thank God for her, or whoever. It wouldn't have been nice. I suggested we look in some hotel parking lots, see if we get lucky.

Nothing. We searched all night. We were really on the hunt and the car was mostly quiet. It wasn't much to talk about, the action would speak louder.

You could tell Cory was scared, but he understood. We were not letting that ride. "Hell nah"

We started all over again the next day. Broad day light hunting now,

111

rumors were, the chicks boyfriend was from this weak little project named Westbrook Village.

We went there. From a distance, we saw a little crowd of dudes standing together. Nate thought he saw at least one of them. I got excited, I wanted to just drive up and kill everybody we could. Fuck it.

But we used our heads. We would wait until we caught them slipping. We left.

Few nights later at the gas station on Main. St., I swore I saw the dude responsible. I was just about to get hum, I was creeping between the pumps, had 2 guns on me. I couldn't just start shooting, gas tanks too close. I didn't want to blow myself up.

He was pumping gas. I tried to get up on him, but this other dude with him saw me. He yelled out, "yo, watch out. Look!" Dude took off. He didn't even finish pumping gas. He pulled off like a bat out of hell. I had him, next time, he's done.

Nate had probation, but he wasn't in violation or anything, until is P.O. saw him on the avenue and tried to grab him. Nate tried to run him over, then took the police on a serious chase. It lasted through 3 towns, they finally got him in Vernon, CT.

He threw his gun, they couldn't find it. They almost killed him, they put more staples in his head.

At court the next day, he passed out. The whole court was in an uproar. He looked bad, I was pissed off. His bond was set at 1 million dollars. He was hit.

He called my house collect that night. He wanted me to try to get him out, but I didn't know how he expected, he really was just stressing. I understand that. But I did get him a lawyer and send him $4000.

That was so he could get relaxed to fight the case. He would have to sit it out. I talked to him every night.

Jacky was scared. All of this shit happening, and the car she rented for Nate was damaged, and the rental car place was going to take it out on her. This dude named Dino that Nate and I knew was doing something in the music world. He met some people and was trying to introduce us, but they were in Florida.

I wanted to call his bluff, so, I'm on my way to Florida. I told Jacky, and she didn't feel comfortable unless we were engaged or something. She didn't trust me going to Florida as a single man.

I had an Idea. She's actually the love of my life. So my decision wasn't a hard one.

I called Quan up, picked James up from school, and we all went to Buckland Hills Mall.

We went straight to Zales, the diamond store.

I asked Quan to pick out the biggest rock he could find. I also searched for it.

I found a nice one, Quan found a bigger one. I asked the lady with the keys to the treasure to allow me to get a closer look of the ring that held my interest.

She reminded me, "that ring is very expensive." I got her cue loud and clear, so I pulled out $10,000 in cash and placed it on top of the counter.

Then stepped out of the shop, held a small conference with Quan and James. Left the money on the counter, James was so excited. He kept saying, "Daddy are you buying that ring for Mami?" I said, "yes," and he responded with, "She's going to like that ring." Quan and I started laughing, "she better."

I paid for it. The nice lady tried to give me a Zales gift card for $200, but I rejected it, told her to keep it. Got a lifetime warranty on the ring though. Anytime a stone fell out, it could be replaced, free of charge. That was nice.

I couldn't wait for my baby to get off work today! James was so excited again. I told him my plans, he almost spilled the beans as soon as she came through the house door.

I kissed her juicy lips as usual, same 2 step, but kept her hostage in the kitchen for a second. The weed was already rolled up and waiting to get sparked.

I got on my knee real quick, all ghetto, and asked her, "yo, will you be my wife?" She snatched the ring and said, "yes." Actually, she snatched the box it was in, when she opened it, she said, "oh my God," and flooded my lips with juicy kisses.

James was clapping his hands, we all hugged. That was a day I'll never forget. I love Jacky.

That week, I flew to Florida. I gave Dino the money and he took care of my rental car, well truck, and I even rented a house for a week. It was nice, had a pool, a jacuzzi, game room, etc.

I met his people In the music business, they were impressed with me. They wanted to sign me to their label, but I still had other work to do. I didn't feel comfortable where my money was, meaning, I needed some more. Shit was getting low.

I missed Jacky so bad, and I was only gone for 2 days. I won't lie, I went out one time in Florida. We went to Pleasure Island, Universal Studios, and at the BET club I popped Crystal for the first and last time. It was nasty.

I felt dizzy as hell in the club. I wasn't a drinker at all, just was trying something new. It wouldn't happen again.

Dino was loving it. He didn't want me to go back to Connecticut. Of course he didn't, I paid for everything out of my pocket. He got a free ride.

I went back to the house I rented and threw up on the nice bed, and just laid there.

The next day I was back on a plane, heading home. My baby picked me up at the airport in the truck and brought me home. We had fun, and smoked. I told her about my trip and how they wanted to sign me. She was happy.

But I was already planning another mission in my mind. I didn't even have a location, but I would soon.

Stakes were getting too high to have Cory hanging with me, but I still had him rent me cars and occasionally we smoked together but shit was about to get crazy again. I could feel it.

Nasia was a cheerleader now, she had this event coming up. She would be a cheerleader at this football game for her school. I had to be there. I missed everything else.

I brought James with me, it was fun. The little dudes played their football game, then the cheerleaders came out. My baby was so cute for her little solo. I was yelling out, "that's my baby." I think she was slightly embarrassed. I'm so ghetto, but I didn't care, I was proud of my baby. That's my girl.

Jacky made me come with her to her mom's house. She wanted to show her the ring. Her moms liked it, and me. She called me, "sugar Daddy". That was so funny, I'm not an old man tricking with a young girl, but I get it. I am Jacky's sugar daddy, and she's the sweetest thing I ever had.

I took my baby shopping. we were in this store called Evelyn's. they had fly shit in there. Of course, I let my baby get whatever she wanted. We didn't have a budget.

This chick that worked there was following us around the store, she worked commission, you could tell. She got excited when Jacky picked out more shit.

I liked watching my baby get what she wanted. It turned me on, she was like a little girl in there, going crazy. I definitely liked the way the other chicks were hawking her down, so jealous. She had that long sexy ass real hair too. I would grab it every now and then and kiss her mouth. Her spit tastes good.

The young girl at the register was ringing out shit up. At the same time, she couldn't take her eyes off of her ring. I caught her staring.

Nate's Maxima finally popped up, but the dudes that jacked it took the rims off. It was found sitting on bricks. I went to get it, and put more rims and tires back on it. It still rode smooth.

I wasn't comfortable keeping it around my crib, knowing suckers took it from my little brother.

I met one of my distant little punk cousins from Day Day side of the family again after not seeing him for a while, My cousin Ty. He hung out on Center St.

He had a driver's license, so every now and then I would let him drive me around. Jacky didn't like him, she felt a bad vibe about him, but I made the mistake and ignored it.

The dude Scott La Rock from my project, the one that ran in the prison when I was defending him. His "neggedy" (sister) saw me on Center Street. We go back to the 90's, we were always cool. She told me her husband Richie had a spot in Waterbury where they lived. It was a booming crack spot, and she wanted me to be his connect.

So I sat with the dude, talked prices and payment plans and it was set. I would supply him. I started copping a Kilo for $18,000 and giving him half of it for $18,000.

18 ounces, for $18,000, it was crazy! Every two days, like clockwork.

I used to have Ty drive me out there, it was safer.

While in Waterbury, I found this little credit union. I needed it, probably get it next week. Ty just kept asking me for money, as if I were some kind of bank. I told him, "next week I'm going to work. I'm bringing you in, you better not let me down."

29 DAMN, DAMN, DAMN

My homework was done. I figured out my routes, etc etc. I only needed Coupeless inside with me, Ty would drive though. I didn't need him at all, I just wanted him to earn a few dollars instead of begging me all the time.

Same old 2 step, stayed out all night and get busy in the A.M. We slept in the car and smoked all night. We went to Richie's crib before showtime.

We would be back after we handled business. Richie's brother Chris would be the second car waiting for us. Ty was instructed, "After its all said and done, take the dirty plate off the rental, put the original back on, and drive straight back to Hartford. Ill meet you later. I got you"

The place opened up at 9am. The safe wouldn't be open until 9:15am. I timed it, we pulled up hoodies tight over our heads.

There was an older couple sitting there in the parking lot. I didn't want to ruin the timing, so we proceeded as if they weren't there.

As we got out, coupeless and I, they looked right at us. No faces exposed, but they knew we were up to no good. They grabbed their phones and started dialing right then and there. My sick self smiled at them. Hopped over this small wooden fence and ran up in there.

I jumped right over the counter, and made everyone back up, not allowing anyone to hit the silent foot alarm. The place was bigger inside than I thought, more tellers, more drawers to empty.

I asked the person nearest to me, "where was the safe?" The lady pointed at it, but said it didn't open for another 3 minutes. Coupeless looked right at me, I knew the woman was telling the truth.

The clock I was going by must have been 3 minutes faster than theirs. So all I could do was eat all the drawers. There were 5 so we still got a nice piece, $110,000.

But it was a Friday! I fucked up, that means the safe could've held a few hundred thousand. Damn, Damn, Damn.

I jumped back over and we left, still great timing. Under a minute flat, we jumped in the rental and I told Ty to run all the red lights. He did, and we made it safely to the other car where Chris was waiting.

Me and Coupeless hopped in with Chris. I told Ty to change the plate, right here and then, nice and calm. Then I told him to head back to Hartford, "make no stops in between."

At Richie's, I started counting all of the money. Richie looking at me like I'm a demon, mouth open, staring at my cash.

When all of a sudden, a knock at the door. I grabbed my gun, Coupeless did as well, Chris went to see what was what.

It was Ty. I was furious! I asked him, "why the fuck aren't you on the highway heading home?"

He said he didn't want to get jerked for his money.

If looks could kill.

I yelled at him, in front of everybody. "We didn't need you. I did you a favor and let you drive just so I could pay you something."

He had the stupidest look on his face. My mind told me, bring him in the backyard and leave him back there.

But I talked myself out of killing his ass. Coupeless definitely wanted to eat him. I gave Coupeless $30,000, gave Ty only $6,000. Lucky I aint give him what my inner self said give him.

I gave Richie $4,000 because I was at his house. I know he wanted more, but he knew better than to ask. $70,000 for me. Not the best, but not the worst.

Got back to the house, stashed a few dollars and hopped in the Yukon. I went to the mall and bought Jacky some clothes and me a few CD's.

I put the stuff in the crib and headed back out. Back at the weed spot, this dude Tone Bone had the Blueberry Haze. I would buy it all every time. As soon as he seen me pull up, he knew he would be sold out.

He use to tell the customers in line before me, "you better get what you can cause, that dude behind you, guarantee you he's buying everything up." He was right.

After he served me, he told me to be careful. I didn't know where he was going with that, but he said that his brother was in the feds with 16 years for robbing credit unions. He had my attention for sure.

Tone Bone said he wondered how I always had too much money. All the time, and now it made sense. Then he added, that my cousin Ty just came through and he was bragging about the job.

I got the chills when he said that. Soon as I left the weed spot, I tried to call Ty. But I messed up, I showed too much emotion and aggression in my voice. Now he's going to duck me.

This was terrible and I had a feeling it was only the beginning.

Then I went down the avenue, seen an old associate and he told me that he heard I been doing big things. I asked him to elaborate, he said, "$175,000, $110,000, etc etc. I tried to convince him it wasn't true, he wasn't biting, said my secrets were safe with him. And that Coupeless was his people, he respect what I was doing for the youth.

Everybody just couldn't keep their trap shut. Now, I would have to shut it for them. If I could catch up with any of them.

They were off to the races, and bringing me with them. Without my consent.

I went home to get my thoughts together, things were getting wild, fast. I had to somehow slow things down.

There was a knock at the door, I opened it fast. It was a federal agent and 2 Waterbury Police Officers. They asked if I was a Jungle, I said, "do you have a warrant for someone named Jungle?" They said no, and I told them to leave.

But before they did, the special agent did some bullshit. He ran through my crib, went upstairs and all that without permission that is, and then he left.

On the way out, they said, "you may not wanna talk, but when we find your young friends, I'm betting they will." Shit!

I peeled off as soon as they left. When Jacky came home, she knew nothing. Then they must have followed me to my moms, they snatched me without a warrant. Basically they kidnapped me.

They got a fake warrant, when I was being held at the Waterbury precinct.

They raided our house. Scared my woman.

They found nothing, but took the new clothes I brought Jacky and even took my old clothes and boots. That was unprofessional, as well as, plain crazy.

They held me in a tight room, which wasn't a cell. By law, they couldn't really hold me at all, they didn't have a warrant for my arrest. But us poor people, mostly foolish, don't know any law and therefore, have no rights.

Before their shift ended, they let me go. I had to wait until Jacky came to Waterbury to pick me up. She was scared, actually terrified, and they talked to her crazy about me.

The FBI outstepped for sure. My case wasn't their's, they had no right to interfere with the investigation.

I had my money stashed at Dawn's uncle crib. I stopped driving my vehicles, I was too hot. I paid a cab driver to take me everywhere. I gave him $400 and he stayed with me until I was ready to go in.

Jacky, James and I stayed one last night together at a hotel. It was very uncomfortable, and my greed had severed my beautiful relationship with the woman of my dreams.

My world came crashing in.

I couldn't come up with any wiser move at the time than to get me a lawyer. I hired this so called high profile lawyer, well known to the system.

That back fired, I won't name his name, the sucker might try to sue me. Anyway, this piece of shit lawyer, initials W.G., I gave him $10,000 and retained him. He said he needed $15,000 if it went to trial. This greedy bastard.

I hadn't even been charged at that point and he already talking trial fees, unbelievable.

A few days later, on Center Street, they got me. They surrounded the whole area, for 4 blocks and rushed in. I tried to make the feds kill me, but they didn't.

They brought me to Jennings Road. Held me at that station, and brought in some homicide detectives. Get this, someone got murdered the night before they got me. They got phone calls from citizens saying it was me.

I wasn't worried at all. After a short investigation, I was cleared of those allegations, but charged with the Waterbury credit union robbery. My bond, well ransom, was $1,000,000. I wasn't going anywhere for a long time.
It gets worse.

30 LOOSE LIPS

I was taunted all night in lock up at the Waterbury precinct. Cops came back and forth, talking all kinds of gangster shit to me.

Arraignment went horribly. My lawyer didn't show up, after that huge retainer fee I dropped on him. His action spoke louder than words, nice and clear. I need my money back ayap!

After court, and the bond is firmly established, then you get sent to your county or high bond reception. I was sent to North Ave, which is Bridgeport's county jail.

This was done to take me out of any possible comfort zone one could establish behind these walls. It would be a strain for my people to visit, and I simply knew no one. No special treatment was coming my way.

They kept showing my face on the news like crazy.

A few times I watched it myself.

Collect calls to Jacky was so painful. She would cry, and this made my eyes watery. She loved me so much, and I loved her so much. If I didn't have her, I might have been numb going through this, but being in love with this beautiful woman. I felt destroyed inside, I never felt that pain. That love!

I went inside the counselors office to take a much needed legal call. When I got through, I couldn't believe the level of disrespect coming my way. Its like everyone knew I was done, and so, I didn't hold any value.

I told my lawyer, since he didn't feel obligated to come to my arraignment, I didn't trust him and to keep $2,000 for nothing and to give the rest to my mother. I would have her come get that, he said, "what money?" Did you get a receipt for that transaction? And hung up on me.

The robber was robbed, by the greasy lawyer, in broad daylight.

I went back to my cell heated. Then get this, the CO's came with cameras and pepper spray ready for me. I didn't understand, they cuffed me and brought me to the medical unit.

Took my clothes, down to the boxers and socks, and replaced them with this Ninja turtle top, bullet proof vest looking joint. My private parts were hanging out, and it was freezing.

That night was crucial, freezing, and they had cameras in the cell watching my every move. You could see the exhale of breath, the room was so cold and basically I was naked.

I had to do pushups and naked jumping jacks to stay warm, and the nurses station was right there. they kept offering me pills for everything and I denied it every time. They were trying to zombie me out.

I couldn't figure out why this was happening, but then it came to light. My fake, grease ball lawyer called the jail and said I was suicidal. He did this, not only to mess with my mental state, but also, to keep me from communicating with the outside world.

It worked, except the having me lose mu mind part. I couldn't make phone calls, hell, I couldn't even eat from a spoon. They gave me a dixie cup as a utensil to eat with.

Then I had to be evaluated to get cleared for general population. Only the psychiatrist had the authority to make it happen.

Just my luck, the one for the facility was out on leave for a family crisis. She wouldn't be back for 30 days.

So I had to sit patiently. It was crazy, "you have no idea," from living my life, lawless by the way, doing whatever I pleased. Smoking good good all day. To being confined to a freezing closet with cameras on me, naked, with pills being offered for a solution.

The morning they gave me back my boxers and pants it took strength I didn't know I possessed not to curse these people out and let them know how I really felt.

They let me get a call, I ran to the phone. Hearing Jacky's voice was like, having life restored to my dead body. It felt that good. I told her what happened with me, she couldn't believe it.

My court date was coming. Finally the shrink showed up, cleared me, back in population. The food annoyed me, the inmates lies were annoying me. Everybody talking like, they were on top out there when you could clearly see with your own eyes. It was nothing like that.

Today I went to the court, more of the same. Still was too early to really know anything. I accepted a court appointed pretender after announcing my lawyers disappearing act.

The dude they gave me had obvious mental issues. He was drooling all over himself, I had to keep asking him was he alright. If he really had a license to practice law, it was a miracle. Or he knew the person administering the test, something.

He kept asking, "where did you stash the money?" with this big greedy lusty smile on his face. All the prisoners in the bullpen with me waiting to go see the judge told me that my lawyer was a big trick in their town. Plus a crack addict. This was believable.

I filed for a motion of discovery. All the information available pertaining to my case, I learned about it being in the cell with Kev from DC. The one that used to rob credit unions.

They cant withhold that information from you, upon request. But you must understand that this is a right, part of due process.

My discovery revealed Ty write a book about me, he also made a video at a hotel stating he did a crime with me and he didn't listen to me. And so, if he got murdered all of a sudden, I'm the guilty one.

He sent one to channel 3 news, and the other, he made for the police.

They believed every word, and Coupeless. He was at his girlfriend's, soon to be baby moms crib, bagging up crack. Music was blasting, weed in the air, guns everywhere. All over the apartment, even in the bathroom.

The special agents, local Waterbury Police and state troopers knocked on his door and asked if they could speak with him. No warrant, he let them in, drugs in plain sight, guns in plain sight, also the weed smoke gave them probable cause.

He was placed under arrest for the stuff in the crib, they asked, do you want to help yourself? You already know what he said, and what he did next.

Started beat boxing and rapping. At the same time, they gave him a trick or treat record deal; and he signed with them.

Not only did they both admit to everything, but they also threw everyone else under the bus and they explained it all in clear details. They signed and sealed our fate, if they but knew.

There was never an arrest warrant for any of their arrests. At any given time, they could have chosen to invoke their rights to remain silent. No cases for any of us.

Coupeless even told on his own brother Quan. I felt bad for Quan, even though my situation was much worst. Quan wasn't into the street life and he was the one, to beg me, to let his brother Coupeless in the circle.

My Jacky knew Ty was a snake all along. I found it out the hard way.

I heard through the system Ty was reversing the roles, and events of things. He played like his life was mine, and mine was his, in efforts to try to make friends in prison. Even that backfired for him when they almost fed that little guppie to this shark.

I saw him, in the midst of getting transferred after court, they slipped up. So I embarrassed him in front of everyone present.

I asked him, why couldn't you just keep your mouth closed. They could've tried their hardest, and they would have never built a case on us.

Then the CO's separated us, and put him on the protective custody seat of the transferring bus, right in front of them, he looked stupid, like a bird in a cage.

A warrant popped for me, for another credit union. These dudes were so confused, they thought that, the more they told, the courts would let them go home.

Boy were they in for a surprise. My bond got raised from $1,000,000 to $2,000,000. Which I didn't care if they raised it to $100,000,000. I couldn't post anything.

I was transferred from North Ave county jail, to Walker Reception in Suffield, the high bond unit. In that spot, we wore yellow jumpsuits and they took my grey and black Gucci sneakers and gave me some karate shoes.

Jacky started coming to see me, she looked so good.

Watching her leave was straight torture. I told her to sell the truck and keep the Bonny. This trouble of mine, really hurt her and I definitely hurt my kids, again. Just when I was getting closer to Kamar and Nasia.

Oh yeah, them suckers also told on Nate. Even though he never robbed any of the credit unions with me, Coupeless told the feds that I gave Nate money from the jobs. He was charged with conspiracy.

People in Walker from Hartford were so jealous and nosey, making comments all the time about how much money I had or didn't have. Like little chicks.

This one cat named Cheese was getting a little disrespectful, so we banged out.

We both went to the box, came out, he went to one side of the jail, and I went to the other.

I guess, some small town kid with a big crime was cool with Cheese, and called himself getting at me.

The CO was from Hartford like me, so he let me and the kid fight in the cell real quick. No real damage was done, the kid kept trying to wrestle with me, I wanted to slug it out.

So the dude was still popping his chops.

My celly was this dude named, Shoes. Shoes was a weird character, not because he got high, but because he always tries to get over on someone. Even if the person is clearly for his betterment. He'll find a way to ruin a good thing.

I knew Shoes for many years in the prison, he also was a scary dude.

This morning he went out, like always, to med call. They called for inmates to get their medications. We were on the bottom tier, the top tier was out on their recreation.

The kid that I fought the other day was on the top tier, he was on recreation. My celly came back, told me the dude wants him to leave the door open so he could come in our cell and fight me.

I started moving things out of the way so if the dude actually came in, we could handle it. I still was a little nervous, the dude was way bigger then me and who doesn't feel like that before a fight.

The dude crept in, closed the cell door shut, my celly curled up on the bottom bunk to be out of our way.

We started banging, bing, bing, bong. Bong, bong, bing, immediately blood was on the scene. I don't know if it was mine or his, but we kept slugging it out, bing, bong, bing.

Shoes picked something up from the floor, he called me, "yo JB, look what he had," it was a shank. I was actually shocked. Oh, this sucker thought he was going to stab me up.

I grabbed the knife from Shoes, went to work with it. Punch him, stab him, stab him, punch him, I did that combination until he couldn't take it anymore. He was squirting like a water gun all in the facial area.

No remorse, I stuck him some more. Then the CO that let us fight the other day, he came to my door. We stopped, and I flushed the shank down the toilet.

Right before the door got popped open, I swung at his face, hard as I could. Cut him, once again. "Yes," I was extra proud of his last wound, all me, all bones.

31 SUPERMAX

The CO said he had to cover his ass by sending the dude to medical, but when he got there they threw him in the hole and immediately launched an investigation. The nurse at medical determined the guy was beaten badly and stabbed in the face. It was true, and so, the CO did what he had to do. He called the squad and they came to get me. While in the hole, I was going back and forth with the dude, yelling from cell to cell. He was claiming the department of corrections was making him press charges on me, but I made him look like a crybaby snitch that came to do damage, but got damage done to him so he refused to press charges on me.

I was taken out of the hole and brought to the captain's office. Other supervisors of DOC were there also. They had pictures of the dude's face and asked me if I myself, wanted to press charges. I just laughed.

Then the captain goes to say, "if you would have killed that guy I would have spoken on your behalf in trial. Since he came into your housing area, he was the aggressor".

Then he further states, do you know what he's in for? I did not, didn't care. The captain says, well he raped and killed his own sister, him and his buddy.

Wow! That was something to know.

They let me out of the hole, because I simply defended myself. I guess, maybe they respected the damage I'd done to him.

Shoes was shocked to see me back in the cell for more than one reason. It appears when the CO's came to pack up my property, all my food was gone. Shoes helped himself to all my food. Regardless of me feeding his broke ass every night.

But with the turn of events, I forgave him. That was just the way it was, he saw an opportunity, I laughed it off. Who knows, had he not seen the shank the guy dropped, maybe I would have been the one stabbed up.

The guys celly was this off brand with dreads, they just showed him on America's most wanted as a captured fugitive. He thought he was some type of celebrity in the Jail. Which he wasn't.

He felt salty over what I did to his celly. He thought his celly was going to tear me down.

I started attending church services. There's no doubt in my mind, God has been saving me from the severest outcomes thus far. Even though I wasn't what you would call a real believer, in a specific way or faith group. I was soul searching.

I started studying the Bible intensely, day and night in search of myself between those pages. I admit, I found some very interesting things. Some of which, I had no doubts were facts of life, beneficial for all mankind, and some I found very contradictive.

I continued the search. Bible study signified a few things. Basic things, but some truth.

I was willing to challenge and debate more than a few topics. In which, the bible study dude wasn't equipped to answer.

Quan just got picked up by the police. My sister Jazzy was so sad. I felt bad for them. His own brother, flesh and blood, did him in.

I couldn't pretend to imagine how that felt. They put him a block over from where I was. His bond was 1,000,000. He was hit too.

Sometimes, I would see him at bible study. Not a lot of people attended. Get this, his brother Coupeless was over there with him, had to be awkward.

I won't lie, I tried to get moved on the side where they were. I was going to fuck Coupeless up for running his mouth, but it didn't happen. That was also God's work.

They moved Nate to Walker also. He was on the side of the jail where I did the stabbing. We were all scattered, but in the same building.

Now my celly was this, cool young kid from New Haven. He played ball and cards a lot. He wasn't looking at too much time but enough to be concerned about.

This was the jail where all the ongoing, high profile cases accused were held.

If someone just got charged with murder, here with us he was. It was a depressing environment, to say the least.

They popped my cell out of the blue, said, pack my shit, I'm moving to the top tier. This was unexpected, I was pissed. Usually, it was hard to end up in a cell with someone you could get along with.

So I moved up top, had no choice anyway. That, or the hole. And in the hole, no phone, no commissary, barely get showers, and you starve.

Soon as I entered the cell it felt like I've been set up. My new celly was an older brother from Waterbury named Raheem.

He was a serious cat, didn't laugh or joke, and he didn't smile much. But really, wasn't much to smile for in our current positions.

I didn't like recreation too much, sometimes I'd go, but most of the time I'd stay back in the cell. I would think about my screwed up life and how I screwed it up.

I would also think about my children growing up without me and Mi Amor, Jacky. I wondered if she moved on already. She was beautiful, I feel blessed to have been her man already.

I missed my moms and my brothers and sisters too. I just got so used to being a lone wolf that I tried to stay numb in my heart; I didn't want to cry. Sometimes I did though, and it hurt, but it felt good too. I was miserable.

I used to watch Raheem pray, and he prayed a lot. I would turn down my TV out of respect to him, but really it was out of respect for God.

He prayed in Arabic, and I found it very interesting. How did he learn that language? Who taught him? Does every Muslim pray that way? Why? Why so many times? Why does he have to wash up before he does? Why, why, why?

All day long I had questions for him, and he'd answered them simply, clearly, and intelligently. Every last question.

Then he often said stuff like, I would be a good Muslim. Why would I be a good Muslim? Me, being good? How could he see this in me? I was a demon. Well, I lived like one for as long as I could remember. I was out of control.

I looked at his Quran, the Muslims holy book. Well, I didn't look inside the pages, I just stared at it. It seemed like it was a bright light, that's how I perceived it.

I thought to pick up that book I would have to learn some different type of manners. Religious manners. A different kind of respect for God. A real respect. And some rules, I wasn't used to any rules in my life.

Raheem was looking at 10 years, and he wasn't a young cat. Late 30's at least. He was still fighting his case.

I went back and forth a few times with myself. The offer in Waterbury was 12 years, I wasn't trying to take that.

I was willing to take 10 years, but they were stern for the 12.

My other case in Hartford courts were really just waiting to see what Waterbury gave me and most likely run theirs along with Waterbury.

I had this private so called lawyer, Hussy. Fake Jewish cat, he cost a lot. He was winning big cases left and right. His name was really popular at the time. I didn't laugh at all at his jokes, they weren't funny to me.

Raheem copped out, meaning he took the plea deal that the state offered. 10 years or go to trial. He didn't trust trial, no fairness, no justice, so really he didn't have a choice.

He got moved to assessment. That's where you went after you got sentenced. He was out, but the message he came with stayed pondering in my heart.

I was watching the news one night; this big gorilla looking cat from Hartford had beat this man down. Almost killed him, they kept showing it on the news until they caught this dude. They had it all on tape.

At this time, I had the cell to myself for like a week. I liked it better this way. I got to think out loud, have good conversations with myself and I could cry whenever I wanted.

Jacky used to still come visit me. She really loves me, even after I took my engagement ring back. I wanted her to marry me, even while I was in prison. Which I know isn't right, but I took it in case I died inside.

I would go a happy man, because the love of my life took me at the bottom of a well and raised my soul up from the dark and cherished it. My body would make it out one day, and love her forever and never let her go.

The thought of her being with another dude almost caused me to lose my mind, and lose hope of life.

This isn't a regular love for me. This is the love of my soul. No other chick is getting this spot again, ever.

It's a one seater, not a coupe.

My cell popped open. You wouldn't believe who they threw in it with me. That same gorilla dude who they just had on the news.

This sucker was 6 feet 6 inches in this little ass space with me.

After he got settled in, we talked. This fool was a Muslim. After a few months, the streets was washing off of him and he got his shine back. He was reading and praying like he should have been.

He transformed right before my very eyes. God rescued him again. He knew the Imam from the streets. The Imam was the person who leads the prayer for the Muslims in the jail. He handled the Muslim's affairs such as services and getting you a Quran.

He held classes to teach the basics. The Imam of the jail was tight with him. He brought him CD's, books, kuffi's for prayer, and things of that nature.

He taught me some things, oh, the giants name was "Ce Co," the C's were pronounced like an S.

He knew how to read and write in Arabic and was actually pretty smart when he cleaned up.

He started teaching me the basics of Islam. So far, so good. He let me read this book he had on "Tawheed"

Tawheed signifies the oneness of God. How HE alone is supreme without any partners or associates. How HE's the ALL POWERFUL, THE MOST GENEROUS, THE ALL WISE.

And, HE's our master and we are HIS slaves. That's one of the main reasons the Muslims bow down to his GLORY in prayer. HE's the only ONE worthy of that.

Then, he showed me proof that they were all doing this in prayer. The proof was right there in the Bible itself.

Abraham, Moses, Noah, Job, Lot and many many more, all of them, peace be upon them all.

This book of Tawheed was unbelievable, meaning, fantastic, and clear. All of the pieces of the puzzle were starting to make sense.

32 ISLAM

My studies continue, and everyday I'm understanding more about life in general, as far as the mission, as far as the purpose is concerned.

The prayers are attracting me in a way I've never been attracted. My spirituality, my soul is turned on.

I haven't touched the Quran yet, because I don't feel that I have earned the privilege as of yet. I'm working my way up, the Quran is my motivation.

I've seen the way Raheem and Ceco ascend when they read the Quran. It appears as they have left earth briefly. I need that.

I learned how the decree of Allah is a preordainment. Allah knew beforehand, what each individual will or won't do with his or her life. He the ALMIGHTY allows the human beings the option, the choice.

I started seeing the 2 highways. One clearly leads to destruction and the other, a peaceful bliss, endless rewards and bounties.

While the path of destruction is paved by glittery trinkets, wild animal desire, greed, selfishness, envy, hate, revenge, ignorance, ungratefulness, violence, corruption, deception, oppression, dealing in fraud, fornication, drugs and alcohol, dishonesty, slandering, falsehood, blasphemy, etc.

Basically, the easy route. While the path for paradise is paved with struggle, good character, charity, prayer, kindness, restraint, discipline, humility, moderation, honesty, integrity, patience, perseverance, submission, surrendering, peace, love, truth, mercy, forgiveness, pain, compassion, sympathy etc.

It's obvious what path I've chosen my whole life, but I'm that learning Allah accepts true sincere repentance and gives respite. An appointed term of life in which one can get his or her stuff together. Basically, make the transition from evil doing to righteous deeds.

I'm about to bet my soul on this thing being true.

I called my baby Jacky, she was telling me what was going on with her and James and how she's scared for us; wondering how much time I would end up doing.

I started to speak and said something pertaining to "my mans and them," and she went in on my. She said, "your mans and them? Fuck your mans and them. You better make God your mans and them. Wow.

She was absolutely right.

I took those words to soul, "make God my mans and them!" and that's exactly what I did from that point on.

To officially start practicing Islam and become a Muslim, you have to take your Shahada which is an oath that you make with God.

You must state that: You bear witness there is only one God, and you bear witness that the prophet Muhammed is his messenger and slave.

After declaring this you are placed under specific obligations such as, five daily prayers. They are prescribed at specific times of the day. They also have to be done in a certain manner of etiquette, such as standing, bowing, prostration, and recitation of the Quran preferably in Arabic.

You also have to fast for 30 days in the month of Ramadon, in a prescribed way.

There is Zakat, which is giving charity.

You also must make the pilgrimage to Mecca, Saudi Arabia at least once in a lifetime if God allows you the means to do so.

It is also required to learn about your faith, about your lord and the humans he sent to humans to relay his message.

I didn't take my Shahada there and then, but I was coming. Ceco was training me hard.

Before I made my vow I wanted a stronger and clear understanding of what exactly I was committing to. I've never felt an inclination this strong to change my life. Enough was enough with this criminal life.

So far, all I've accomplished with it was to hurt my children who god blessed me with, my family, and this new final love of my life in Jacky.

Any and everyone who has ever invested feelings, thoughts or emotions in me. I cant do it anymore.

I was learning the posture of the prayer, as well as, how to say it in Arabic. I admit, the Arabia was intimidating me, after all, I'm only a sixth grader at best.

I wanted it for my soul, and so I made a vow. I asked God if he made it easy for me to digest, I'll dedicate my life in prayer and with sincerity. I would be one of his best striving slaves in these days and times. I meant these vows from my soul.

God knows best what his servants intentions are.

The Quran says, God is closer to you than your jugular vein. I believe that wholeheartedly.

God answered my prayers. I learned my prayers in Arabic and actually enjoyed praying. I really do, it feels good.

Since Friday is the best day of the week in the Muslim world, that's when I took my Shahada. Right after Jumua, the day of assembly or gathering.

Muslims learn that God, THE ALMIGHTY created all life on Friday and that will also be the day of judgement. Only God knows exactly when this is to take place so beware of your deeds. Everything small or great is being recorded for this day to come.

I have a lot of work to do. God willing I'm able to exchange all my bad deeds for good ones.

A code was called on Nate's block. I had a bad feeling that he was involved. Sure enough, he was. These 2 punks jumped him. He was hurt, but he survived.

After he came out of the hole, they moved him to my block. The cell right under mine, we could talk through the ventilation system.

I couldn't stop talking about AL-Islam. Every time the conversation got serious I had to excuse myself, it was time to pray again.

Even when it was time for my recreation, I would go talk to Name about AL-Islam. Eventually, he agreed to check it out. At that time he was an Atheist, be he said he would give it an optimistic research.

After maybe a months journey in study, he also took his Shahada. I was happy like a father would be at his own son's graduation.

He learned how to pray also, he was holding it down. Even though we were still in hot water, the new faith in God made everything tolerable.

But let me tell you, with that slipping out of the devil's grip, came some new trials. No my faith would be tested all through my prison sentence.

They say, "Faith without work is fruitless."

The DOC supervisor, whom I've had problems with in the early 90's was still holding a grudge towards me and couldn't wait for the opportunity to abuse his so called authority. Someone snitched on me and said that I keep shanks in my cell. This is a serious crime within the prison system in which they act upon swiftly.

So, one early morning, I was fading in and out watching this Spanish talk show when I happened to look towards my cell door. I was about to get raided, they were creeping up.

So I jumped off of the top bunk, grabbed the shanks, and went to flush them. The door was already popped open, so I had to tussle with that supervisor to hit the flush button.

I hit it, but he tried to put his hand in the toilet and grab the shanks. So out of reflex, I elbowed him in the face. His toy soldiers called code orange, which is the code when a DOC staff is assaulted.

They rushed in deep, maced the shit out of me and tried to tackle me down, but couldn't. Everyone was coughing. The inside of the cell was only but so big.

My celly and the CO's were choking hard.

My eyeballs felt like they were burning out of the sockets.

By standard procedure, they were supposed to bring me to medical and flush the pepper spray out of my eyes. But they made me suffer for my actions.

I went straight to the hole, like a basketball player. Prayer time came, and I still made my prayers. I would be getting transferred to the supermax when the hole time was done.

This wouldn't stop me from practicing my faith but was definitely an obstacle.

The supermax was called Northern. This is where they housed death row inmates, gang bangers, and any of the violent prisoners. This was the dungeon, seriously. They stripped me of my property. No really, they broke my TV, took my photos of my family, my Jacky, and my kids. They also took my underclothes and food. Whatever I had was gone.

They did me dirty and then made me stay in a cell with the cuffs on with just my Underwear. It was so cold. What they did to me before with that suicidal watch shit was much more intense and painful to endure, but this pain was similar.

After a day, they gave me a jumpsuit and started treating me like a human. But this place was designed to break you down mentally. I'm sure Guantanamo has a similar structure.

I went to court in Waterbury. I decided to take the ball out of my so called co-defenders court. They were all banking on me to go to trial so they could testify against me and get a deal from the state.

I ruined all that. I took the 12 years and ended all of my Waterbury court trips. That was over for me, also the other credit union robbery. It all ran together.

However, for the fake assault on the DOC supervisor, I got played. Major. I was willing to admit guilt, just to have this over with and move on with my life, but I plead to the charges and for it to be served concurrent with 12 years that I already had.

But when I came for sentencing it was a different judge. He was supposed to honor the plea with concurrent time, but instead he talked crazily about me and to me. Then, he forced me to take a consecutive sentence.

This turned my 12 years into 16 years. I fought it for some years, but as my faith got stronger and stronger, I just made the best of my time and worked on myself.

I strived to be a better Muslin and to bury my old life of crime. I finally get it, but it took severe pain. I'm hurting.

33 TEST OF FAITH

I talked Jacky into moving to Florida. She is beautiful, intelligent, young and fresh. I didn't want to hold her back from becoming an even more successful woman than she already was.

What made me love her even more was the fact that she would have stayed in CT, visited me the whole bid, and put her life completely on hold. All for me. I know this for a fact.

But that would have been unfair. As much as I am in love with her, my faith in God was teaching me to finally stop being selfish. The moves I made was affecting other people's lives.

I heard Nate took 7 years, and all the cats that pint the finger at me still got smoked in court. I wasn't happy at their outcome, but I wasn't losing any sleep.

I made it out of the supermax and my level dropped down to maximum security. They sent me to this racist spot called Corrigan. It was in Uncasville, CT. listen to the name, "Corrigan, Uncasville," crazy right?

Intake alone made me feel like I was in a refugee camp. I got 16 years, 3 in already and they got me mixed in a big bullpen with dudes serving 30 days for DUI's.

After intake and medical clearance, I was sent to A block, which is orientation block.

Top tier, bottom tier, just like the other max joints. As soon as the new arrivals came into the block, all eyes automatically on you and your property.

The appraisal begins. People love to clock your math, see if you got food, TV, CD player, etc.

If you have lots of shit people will come out of the woodwork and help you carry your stuff to your cell. This way, they think you're their friend and not the request line is open.

Trust me, if they helped you with all your shit, they're coming soon afterwards.

I was in the cell with this funny looking black dude, he didn't have a mustache. He was a jailhouse worker. He did cleaning on the cell block, so he had different types of privileges. Shit I never want.

I unpacked my stuff which I was in the process of rebuilding after the CO's robbed me for my property.

My new celly was from New Haven, an older dude. He was trying to make small talk, but I wasn't really with it. So for the sake of not being rude, I let him see my new pictures. Usually, when you transfer in somewhere it takes at least a few hours to get settled. My stuff was unpacked, but you only stay in the orientation block for 30-60 days. Then you moved to another block.

After showing my photos, I guess my celly felt obligated to show some as well. Again, this didn't interest me, but I didn't want to me rude. His photos looked crazy to me. I kept those thoughts to myself.

This dude had life. I stopped in the middle of our conversation and pardoned myself to make a prayer.

When I finished, the old fool told me he used to be a Muslim and then starts to recite some Quran in a beautiful melodic tone. I was completely shocked and confused. Confused because in the short time that I had been practicing Islam, I knew this was a game changer for me.

So for this old dude to tell me he was a Muslim, past tense, and no longer honors truth and basically feels no obligation to bow down before his master. I felt sick to my stomach.

Then he reveals to me his medical status, which he had full blown aids. He even passed it down to his children, whom he said were living with a lot of difficulties due to that.

I couldn't wait to get out of that cell. I wasn't staying there for 30-60 days, no way. I need out now!

One of the supervisors was doing his tour. Walking through the block, making sure everything was running smoothly. When he got to my cell, I stopped him. I told him, "listen, I'm Muslim, my celly's gay. This cant be my living quarters. I'm very uncomfortable.

Even if I had to go to the hole, so be it. The supervisor already knew my name and that I just got out of the supermax. He knew I was a probationary period from the supermax that entailed, if I got into any trouble within 60 days, I would get sent back. Immediately. This was news to me.

He gave me his word that tomorrow I would be moved to B block, which was nicknamed the body block. It was the lifer's block. Almost everybody there had life or just about. My 16 years was considered a short stay there.

My celly on B block, another weirdo, Spanish brother, swore he knew the Bible. He didn't know shit. Plus, he would do backflips if drugs came on the block.

He didn't appreciate me always praying. He said Muslims pray too much. No real person of any faith would make such a ridiculous comment.

No man woman or child could pray enough. We owe our lord a debt that we could never honestly repay. What's the cost for life? It's priceless.

What would a blind man pay for sight? Or a deaf man pay for his hearing? These are only a few things, very significant, but who can count the bounties and favors God has bestowed on each individual?

Now this cell went to the supervisor and requested for me to be moved. So now I was moved 2 cells down. This Jamaican kid from Hartford was my celly now. A cool cat, we got along well. He was into the Bible.

What I respected about his understanding of the Bible, was that he knew we had to bow down to our lord and that there is only one God. He not only bowed down to his lord in prayer, but he also observed the sabbath every week.

Which is really from Friday's sunset to Saturdays sunset. A lot of people were confused in that manner, but he knew.

He didn't have money to buy food, but he knew how to cook the food up real nice. He made it taste like food from earth. So I bought it, and he prepared it.

Being that we both had faith, we recognized our situations as blessings from the ALL MIGHTY. And we were thankful. There were 15 so called Muslims on B Block. I say so called because a lot would say they were, but what their actions spoke was something crazy.

I met this brother named Jamil. He'd been Muslim before he came to prison he says. He had 22 years, was in for 11 already. God blessed him to have a parole date coming up soon even though he had only been in half of his sentence.

He was on the bottom tier. I was on the top tier. That was where all the people he knew lived. The tiers didn't mix like that so he was requesting to move upstairs in the cell with me. He knew I prayed a lot, studied, and knew I had money.

My celly, the Jamaican dude was a cool cat and although we had different faith affiliations, our faith was similar.

I really didn't want to switch celly's but Jamil made a good Islamic point. When 2 or Muslims pray together, you get 27 times the blessings that you would normally get from an individual praying alone.

So for that reason alone, I accepted the move, but I had a feeling that I would regret it.

We made the move today, let's see how it goes. Jamil had a lot of property. 11 years worth of shit. He had some great Islamic books that I couldn't wait to read.

He had a 10 volume set of Sahih Bukhari, which is Ahadith, reported traditions of the Prophet Muhammed. Peace be upon him.

It was about the way he conducted his affairs Islamically and resolved issues through the community. Basically, his sublime morals and character as the leader of the faithful and the messenger of god.

Helping Jamil move in was a job. I should've got paid for that. One of the prayers came in between the time of the move, the middle one called ASR.

We believe, its when the angels change shifts. From the heavens to the earth and vice versa. Although all of the 5 daily prayers are significant, this one holds extra value. I couldn't wait to make it together and get 27x the blessings.

I asked Jamil was he ready to pray, he said, "nah. I'll do mine by myself later." I almost fell out, this was already a terrible sign.

The next prayer after ASR was called, "Mahgrib" or the sunset prayer. I asked him, are you ready to make prayer? Again, he rejected.

That whole day went by. Nothing, but he did ask me over and over if I wanted to cook something to eat.

It was said, Jamil cooked really well. I wasn't concerned with that. The reason he moved in, I thought was to get blessings and benefit from being in the cell with another Muslim.

He played Gameboy faithfully. Now that's what he did do. Day and night. He only stopped to eat, barely slept, but that Gameboy was on.

I was pissed off. It would have been better to stay in the cell with the Jamaican Christian dude. At least he did practice his faith, and he had a better character.

On top of this dude Jamil being whack, he was loud as can be! People would come to my cell door to talk with him while I was praying.

He should've known better. He was extremely rude.

He also loved hanging around gang members. I mean, he could talk about their codes and break downs all day, without a pause.

May god forgive me, Jamil was garbage.

34 PATIENCE

Days were the same, in and out. Jamil was more annoying by the second/ he went to parole this week and got it. First, he claimed that he didn't make it, then the truth came out.

His level dropped to medium security, so he got transferred. That was music to my ears. Even though he would be going home soon, he was so greedy, asking if he could have this and that. Knowing that I had a journey ahead of me.

I gave him my brand new beard trimmers. The begging got to me, but it stopped there. He was asking for 2 of my brand new Kuffis I just got sent in. that was out, my moms sent me those so they held a sentimental value.

Every now and then I got disciplinary reports and would lose certain privileges. I got sent to the ticket block. This is where all the so called knuckle heads would go.

I was over there for a while. You wouldn't believe who had become my celly again. Raheem, the first Muslim celly I had in Walker.

As soon as he walked in the cell, I greeted him Islamically which is, as salamu alaikum. And he responded back wa laikum as salam. Then after that he said alhamdu lilah. And I repeated it.

A few hours later, it was time for the 5th prayer. The last one for the night, called Eesha. We made it together, side by side. Like it was supposed to be done. 27x the blessings, I needed those.

Raheem was surprised at how much I learned about Al Islam since the last time we were celly's. we talked about Islam almost all day every day.

He still maintained a productive routine. Prayed and studied, then prayed some more. He packed on a few pounds, but he was a big dude to start with.

At that time, I couldn't read in Arabic so I still read the Quran every day in English. I knew my prayers in Arabic and I strived to perfect those joints daily.

Raheem used to read the Quran in Arabic beautifully and I would sit down and listen as a student would. It was almost mesmerizing, the melodies of each chapter.

I was hoping to be on that level one day. In Al Islam, we learn not to be presumptuous in regards of time. Nobody knows what day will be their last. So we cover the bases by saying, "insha allah" for almost everything worth saying. For it is all being recorded for a day of account.

Raheem had great discipline when it came to certain things, but not when it came to food. He would eat you out of a house and home if given the opportunity.

He got old man cranky when he was hungry. Out of 114 chapters in the Quran, he knew maybe 50 by heart. This made him somewhat arrogant.

I was doing a lot of voluntary fasting at the time and I couldn't actually eat food or drink water until sunset, so I saved my food up for later.

On the block we were on, you didn't eat in a mess hall or cafeteria setting. You ate in the cell. While I was fasting during the day, Raheem ate all his food. At night, I would eat mine. He would stare at me, this was extremely rude, as well as uncomfortable and annoying.

Then, I'd offer some of it to him. He'd eat it all, and still be staring asking if I was going to eat the bread or mushy pudding.

Then a lot of youth were getting interested in Al Islam, and I would teach them the little I knew. Basically the basics, and Raheem would get jealous of that. He would say stuff like, "damn, can I get some of the blessings too?"

Meaning, can I teach some of these people too, but there were coming to me and God allowed me to relate with the youth and break things down in a more digestible manner.

I was enjoying my faith, and therefore, to speak on it boosted my energy and metabolism. It felt good.

Just like real brothers, we got into arguments, but never fought. Eventually, he moved out of the cell. It didn't matter.

I got cleared to go back to B block. They put me in an empty joint for like a week, then they slid in another weirdo.

The cats name was Dreon. He was a practicing jew, so called. I say that because he had a serious problem with paranoia. He was in for murder, he had 35 years and was at 16 flat at the time. He had been through a lot. I felt sympathy for him, to an extent.

He accumulated lots of books on Hebrewism. I admit, he introduced me to a lot of truth. I learned in fact that I am a Hebrew.

It's not a religious group, but an ethnicity. Hebrew means burned skin people. Jesus, peace be upon him, was a Hebrew. Soloman, David, Abraham, Moses, the list goes on. Even the prophet Muhammed recognized that he also had Hebrew blood. His father was an Arab, while his moms, Aminu was in fact an Ethiopian woman.

All the prophets in the Bible, Torah, and Quran were all Hebrews part of the 12 tribes, the children of Israel. People aren't taught this, for the purpose of maintaining division amongst the tribes. It goes with the saying, "united we stand, divided we fall." Or, "divide and conquer."

I am a Hebrew that practices Al Islam. I am Muslim, I have African blood, Latin blood, and its all human being. Out of 12 tribes of the children of Israel, at least 8 of them are latin.

Our people need to know this, but we don't. although Dreon taught me a lot about my ancestors, he showed extreme jealousy towards me in our cell.

I would pray and study consistently all throughout the day, and enjoy it. All while Dreon would be bugging out, literally going crazy over his medication and whispering in the cell. He would point at his TV saying the feds bugged it.

His extensive accumulation of knowledge, and lack of use, I believe has basically turned him into a mad scientist. Like the saying, "use it or lose it."

35 BACK TO THE SUPERMAX

Dreon was taking trips to medical every couple of hours. He used to speak with the mental health personnel, then come back to the cell worst than he left.

I think also, what scared him the most is that I really have faith so he couldn't intimidate me in any form. We almost fought a few times, and I could see it in his eyes. He was scared.

The night before, he used the razor in the cell. You'd have to request for razors, then bring them back to the CO's once you finished. I gave him privacy when he shaved, in hope that when I needed one, he would return the courtesy.

For some odd reason, I didn't trust him, like he was plotting something. Sure enough, my gut feelings were right.

After he went to see mental health, I got raided in the cell. They ripped through all of our things, but it wasn't random. It was requested, they were looking for something specific. They didn't find it, whatever it was.

I figured it out, Dreon was setting me up. It wasn't working. When I returned to the cell, I immediately saw a shank in the light fixture, hanging. I guess God blinded the cops sight when they were looking for that. It was right in their faces.

So to ruin Dreon's plans further, I called the CO to the cell before I cleaned the mess up, I showed him the shank hanging in my light. "that's what you were looking for huh?"

He took the shank and told me the obvious, which was, Dreon was trying to get me knocked off. He told the mental health staff that I had weapons in the cell. That's why they came searching.

Since his plan failed, he was exposed. The CO's were coming for his property. He was getting transferred. Hours later out of the blue, I was getting transferred.

The DOC set me up to get Dreon. How?

They know what he did, and since it didn't work, they threw him to the sharks. They put us in the same bullpen in hopes that I would hurt this dude.

He was swearing on everybody dead in his family that he didn't set me up. Only reason I didn't scrape him was because I didn't want to give the DOC what they wanted.

I got transferred to Gardener CI. I was there before. The facility had become majority mental health and only 2 blocks housed regular prisoners. A block and E block. I was on A block. I accumulated a lot of property again, so as soon as I came on the block, the appraisal began.

Dudes put no cut on it, staring at your shit raw through them plastic bags. First couple of cats wanted to help me with my bags. I told them, no thanks, I got it "shot blocker".

You wont score one free throw around here. It's unbelievable how these cats try to be cool to get food. It would take at least 2 hours to unpack and settle in. So I slid to the ping pong room to make prayer.

As soon as I finished, I noticed a little rap cipher. Dudes were okay, but no match. I almost went in, but decided, I'm here, there will be other times. I had to get settled in, and leaving your property blocking the cell was a no no.

I didn't even know who my celly was at the time.

It took about a hour and a half. Things were situated. My celly was this dude named Smalls, Waterbury cat. He had 14 years for trying to rob a bank. He had no bank robbery skills, but he did have weed. This cat had dumb weed, like he was in the street.

As soon as the CO came through doing his count, Smalls lit up a spliff. It smelt good, taste good, felt good. I made my prayers and know that, though no one could be perfect, Al Islam is a blessing. I'm not giving up Islam, for nothing.

I opened the Quran, and realized, the punishments in the hereafter are truly severe indeed, but the rewards for striving in righteous deeds was mind blowing.

Eternal life, in bliss, no more pain, no more suffering, no aging. No losing basically, it's all a win. I need it, I beg God to make me strong enough to make the transition. I have work to do.

Jacky's way in Florida, 1500 miles away, but I love her like she's standing right beside me. Crazy right?

She spent a fortune on my collect calls. $25 a pop, and didn't make me feel like shit for it, even though I did on my own. I hated being without her.

Sometimes I would just fantasize on how she felt and loved me so good. And looked into my eyes and did whatever I asked with no delay. And I cry. I don't care if people think I'm weak over her. I love Jacky, she's my soul.

I knew God wasn't going to let me remain in the cell with the dude Smalls much longer. He was getting reckless on the block, got sent to the hole. So I had the cell to myself for a few weeks.

It gave me some time to think out loud. Reflect. I studied, prayed, and cried more intensely. I need my life to be more than what it's been. I'm in the process of reinventing, it's a struggle, but by the grace of god, I can, and will do it. God willing.

I can't believe I'm still alive. That alone has to be proof of me having bigger fish to fry.

I got a new celly, Spanish cat named Conqueror, it didn't matter to me what name he chose, I wasn't calling no man that. He was from Bridgeport, gang banging dude, told lies all day and couldn't possibly think I believed one word he said.

He was skid bidding, meaning, he was in and out swiftly. I didn't look forward to communicating with him, he spoke English, but narrowed his word play down to a few measly insulting, ignorant words.

One night, he nitpicked an argument over the dumbest shit.

I gave him the automatic silent treatment, he couldn't take it. So in response to be not responding, he said something slick. I checked him so hard he begged the CO to take him out of my cell.

He ended up making a commotion and got sent to the hole. But check this, it happened again.

They came to raid me, and this time, said they found a razor in the cell. It wasn't mine, but a prisoner's word holds zero weight on the scale. They sent me to the hole.

After a week, I came back to the block. Same spot, no celly. I regathered myself, I was being tested by the devil immensely.

The razor was put there by my old celly, this was becoming a regular occurrence.

Going to the hole does something to you mentally and if I didn't have faith to hold on to, I probably would have been out of my mind.

This has been a mental challenge with me, since the days of long lane.

I was getting back on track, then, out of the blue I'm getting transferred back to Corrigan. When it comes to being transferred, it's not an option. You either go shackled and walk on the bus yourself, or you get shackled and dragged on the bus. But you go.

Back in Corrigan, this time, no orientation. They sent me straight back to B block. Here we go with the weirdo celly adventures. My celly name was Will, extra bugged the fuck out. He was from New Haven, he actually was pretty good when it came to the law.

If the DOC came at him incorrectly, he was known to make staff members pay out of pocket. So they walked on eggshells around him. Plus, this dude knew how to box well. He was known for that, his specialty was attacking people.

I won't lie, I had him briefly train me, he taught me some combinations. Deadly stuff. Anytime I had the cell to myself, I would practice harder. Mostly when he went to the law library or to get his medication.

My favorite was the right, left, right, then switch it. And watch that footwork. My grandfather was a Heavyweight Champion Boxer, so I knew I had it in me. "Wiliam Champ Ward" he's documented officially. My mom's pops.

What Will got out of the deal training me? An official celly. I shared food, and kind of talked him out of knocking people out. Trust me, he needed that. Only thing I hated about him being in the cell was his cousin Jihad, Muslim dude, always came around. He knew how to box good as well, but he was a tyrant. Bullied his celly's, made them cut their TV's off at a certain time, and threatened them.

Oh yeah, he had 40 years, was only in 8. He did a precious 25 year bid. Didn't get out until after 18, went home and fell in love with a stripper. Then killed a dude for disrespecting her. Now he's mad at the world.

The reason why I hated when he came around, he was always trying to recruit me. I wanted no parts.

He used to beef with other Muslim's in prison, to the extent he would come to our prayer service with shanks.

A lot of people didn't know that. But, because Will was his cousin, he brought that bullshit around me. I felt trapped sometimes.

I was cool with this Muslim brother of mine named, Mustafa. He was from the Bronx, he had 14 years. Mustafa had a little pull because he worked in the property room.

So he got me moved in the cell with him. Jihad and Mustafa had a feud that shouldn't exist, but it had. Jihad was fuming, starting beef with the whole block. There were 15 or better Muslims on B block and they all hated Jihad. He also used to rape white boys. This isn't a rumor.

He cut off his eyebrows, he was looking crazy and everybody knew he had a knife on him.

Mustafa was a good dude, far as the eye could see, he loved being a Muslim but struggled with his love for something else. He use to gang bang as did I, but I dropped mine like a hot potato. Every day his old people tried to keep him in.

Young boys would come by our cell and always ask him about the history of things and somehow he felt compelled to enlighten them. He had to learn himself, this would come back and bite him.

But it bit us both. Jihad told some people we were running the Bloods, this wasn't true, but like I said, a prisoner's word means nothing unless it was about another prisoner.

So we got put in the hole, on investigation. That lasted as long as they allowed, then the process got repeated. 30 days in the hole. For nothing. I had to stop being angry, but my prayers never stopped. My faith is always being tested, but I know God got me.

36 STAYING STRONG

They let Mustafa out of the hole first, then me days later. Mustafa was transferred out. I was sent back to B block. I hated that, but it is what it is.

I was in the cell with this dude from New Haven. Homeboy should've chosen a basketball career, he was too tall to commit crimes. Too easy to catch.

It's crazy because this tall fool was a gang banger and not the brightest bulb. This is the person I get placed in a cell with.

Besides him being a fool, I knew there was something more odd about his character. I had a bad feeling.

I was on the top tier, Jihad was on the bottom tier, but he kept sending me messages like he was still out to recruit me. "No thank you."

The block got raided at least twice a year. Annual shake downs. The CO's would come in and tear up your cell, rummage through your shit. They would leave no stone unturned.

So everybody, from the top tier to the bottom got sent to the gymnasium. We would stay until the shakedowns were done. Usually, we'd be there for 5 – 6 hours. Crazy.

I hated shake downs, it made you so uncomfortable. I'm already in prison and now I'm subjected to zero respect. Does something to the mind.

I was on the bleachers, minding my business. Some people played basketball, some cards, some chess or checkers, etc.

I went over to the corner spot and laid down on my prayer rug. faced northeast to Mecca, to the best of my ability, and prayed my afternoon prayer. It's called DHOR, pronounced, "Thor." Our second of 5 daily prayers.

In the midst of it, I felt the police presence. I was surrounded by at least 8 CO's. I continued to pray. I admit, it was very distracting, but I focused as much as God would allow me under the circumstances.

They had to be pissed off, I usually took about 15 minutes for this particular prayer. I didn't feel the need to speed up, so I didn't.

As soon as I finished, they cuffed me, they had the camera on me the whole time. Even while I prayed. I kept asking, "what did I do?" but the CO's supervisor said, "don't worry, you'll find out soon enough!"

They took me straight to the hole. Later on I found out why. I was charged with Gang Affiliation. I stayed in the box fighting the charges for 60 days. Meanwhile, I maintained my faith, still made my prayers and every time they placed a person in the cell with me, I spoke to them about god and Al Islam.

God knew I wasn't in the gang stuff anymore, and so, I figured that I must have a mission to complete somewhere, wherever they chose to send me after this ordeal is settled.

A few nights in the cell I was in, it was freezing cold. But I didn't let that hinder me in the least from making my prayers. They say, "what don't kill you, make you stronger."

They convicted me of being a gang member and sent me back to the supermax. God has something planned for me. They put me in a cell with this Spanish kid from Waterbury, named Carlos. He was a marine, and a fake soft ass gang member. A Latin King, so called.

He lucky I didn't knock his ass out, just for being that. But that would've been the old me. The man I'm striving to be has to look past that. My schedule scared him. I did extra prayers in the early hours of the morning, consistently. Since he did tours in the middle east, he wasn't accustomed to seeing Muslims on US soil with the zeal.

We spoke about his military career, briefly. He told me how they ordered him and others to kill everything moving. Women, children, whoever. He said he wasn't proud of it, but when I asked if he would go back, he said yes.

So for that answer, fuck him.

We didn't remain celly's for too much longer. He was scared of me, so he begged the unit manager to get him out of there, and they did.

I had the cave all to myself. Great studying, praying, solitude and conversations. I was reminded of how the Prophet Muhammed, peace be upon him, was in the cave and the angel Jibril (Gabriel), peace be upon him, came to see him.

I took advantage of this alone time. I also had one or two of my favorite visions in that cave.

The month of Ramadon came and I started my fasting. I met a good brother Yasir, from Sudan. He was the Imam who came from outside the walls. He worked for the DOC, but he has compassion for Muslim brothers in the can. He would bring books and good advice, all the time. I always keep him in my prayers.

Our recreation is held in open space, where the top and bottom tiers have a full open view. The phones were on the side of the wall and 3 showers in plain view with glass and a metal door.

Outside of recreation, has a hoop in a very tight space in which even the view of the open sky is blocked by wire.

I already showered, and was making my Mahgrib prayer, when two rivals had a small riot. Trying to remain focused on what I was doing, I still heard punches connecting to flesh. From the sound of things, you just knew blood was on the scene.

The Goon Squad, or Ninja Turtles, however may you a acquire the vision, came rushing in. camera's rolling. Everybody was on the floor cuffed up. Well, except me that is. I kept praying.

They yelled first, but when they realized that I wasn't budging and they couldn't touch me, they stood and watched. I took my time.

The prisoners remained on the floor until I finished, even the injured cats.

As soon as I finished, they rushed everybody back to their cells. They was talking shit to me along the way back to my cell. I told them fools, "fuck your protocol. I'm a Muslim.

Oh, they didn't like that.

They made us participate in all kinds of programs. This wasn't optional. The only way to leave the Gang block and go back to general population was to successfully complete all of the programs.

I did what was required of me, and nothing more. The state of Connecticut was in the process of changing up a few things regarding the supermax. So the whole block I was on was getting transferred to Corrigan. That was the new spot for the Gang block.

I had good reason to hate being in Corrigan, that's where they always set me up. Even where they falsely affiliated me at.

I was in a single cell in Northern, those days were gone. In Corrigan, on the new Gang block, I had a new celly. A cat from Brooklyn. He was a Crip, on his way to the fed joint.

We got along alright, but he told lots of lies. On the Gang block there was a lot of fights, all the time. People even put hits out, cell to cell. Meaning, small notes would get passed from cell to cell to instruct a member to launch an attack.

Either on their celly, or someone they had recreation time with.

The so called team, that my celly was with were the minority. But they had the most heart from what I saw. I heard them yell out some of their secret codes of and knew something was about to go down. "sure enough."

They must've timed it, cause exactly whatever time it was, 3 different assaults took place. All Crip work.

The way the DOC had it setup, they would mix different gangs up in the cell. Sometimes it was peaceful, most of the time, their little trick worked. Blood everywhere.

I finished the program and was waiting to get my papers from the commissioner's office; so I could return back to general pop.

Meanwhile, some funny business was taking place. Every couple of days, they were raiding someone's cell and magically finding a certain size knife.

So when they came to raid our cell, I knew honestly, there was nothing to worry about. But there was this racist CO named Turner. Nothing was honest about him, except, he was honestly a racist pig.

Ain't this some shit, he finds a knife. Me and my celly are cuffed up and brought to the box. Oh yeah, then separated.
"God help me."

37 GOD IS THE GREATEST

So now, I'm in the box. Kind of stressing. I had officially finished the gang program and was only waiting for my acknowledgement papers from the commissioner. This allows me to return to general population.

Now this happens, and I really was set up. If found guilty I would get an outside charge. This would add more time to my already lengthy sentence of 16 years.

I prayed more concentrated, I even cried during prostrations. Begging my lord, please don't let these people defeat me with false heart.

"Please god, but if this is your will please make me strong enough to endure it. Please god let the truth prevail."

The day of my make or break hearing, in regards of the knife. I kept begging my lord. "Please help me."

I had to stand before a panel. The average prisoner maybe would have been terrified in my situation. But no matter what, I knew I had God. That was my strength.

A speaker said to me in a low tone, almost whispering, "what were you just doing over there? praying?" and I told him, "always."

That same speaker announced aloud for the entire room to hear. "Something just happened in this room that none of us can logically explain. Which was, the knife in question, had just disappeared in thin air. Like poof"

Everyone turned their attention to me. I smiled, then chanted repeatedly. "Allahhuakbar, (God is the greatest) Alhamdulil Lahee Rabil Alamin." All praise to God lord of the worlds. Mashallah, it is as God wills it to be.

I was so excited, and with good reason to be. They had to tell me to shut up, but I didn't. and so that day, I returned to general pop.

Back to B block, once again. Some say, third time's the charm. Let's see.

I was put on the bottom tier in this cell with this old Spanish man, he was alright. People told me, he was a pedophile, but I think, he knew better than to try me in that cell.

I established my prayers immediately. There was no confusion or misunderstanding what faith I practiced.

The dude gave me my space.

It was Friday, I was fiending to go to Jumuah, the Friday assembly prayer or gathering of the Muslims.

Hours before Jumuah, I was summoned to the Captains office. I didn't like that, nor did I trust it. Immediately, I was summoned and told that an inmate told them I would probably stab them if we saw each other at Jumuah.

I knew who this person was and was surprised he was so scared to see me. After all the shit he'd been talking behind my back. Plus, he had life in prison.

This was a curse it appeared, but a blessing came out of it. Since they basically ambushed me and told me they had to transfer me on the spot.

Check this, God blessed me to have my level drop from maximum security to medium security. So I went to the jail next door of Corrigan. A level 3 called Radgowski.

This was an entirely different prison setting than I had gotten used to. It was all open dorms. No cells, in cubicles.

They had a microwave. The dayroom TV had basic cable. They even had an Iron. I was bugging. Without really noticing, this was a sign that time was flying. I was getting closer to freedom, but the journey still exist and without faith in God, I'm done.

I met a good dude named Don. He had the same last name as me, and was from Hartford as well. He had 20 years. I talked to him about Al Islam, he was a good listener.

I called Jacky, it's been a while. Going through all the supermax and gang block shit and the setups by the DOC. It had me really watching my surroundings.

It was so good talking to her but I could tell her heart was still mine, but her body wasn't. I love her so much, but I left her by coming to prison. I didn't want her to be miserable.

She disappeared on me. No number, no address, no communication whatsoever. I was crushed inside, but I had to remain strong. If God really gave her to me, she'll be back. Back to stay.

I stayed in Radgowski without incident for a year.

Out of the blue I got transferred. They sent me way out in the sticks. This real racist child molester private jail they called Brooklyn. A lot of people didn't mind being there, because they had ice cream, pizza and soda on the weekends.

I didn't care about that stuff. This was also a dorm setting, basically same setups as Radgowski, just smaller.

The first night there, early hours in the morning. I used to do extra prayers. That was my daily routine, no matter where I was, or the situation.

So I found a nice clean spot in the corner, made my prayers and attempted to go back to my cube. When the CO called me to the "Bubble", which is their station.

He asked me, what was I doing in the corner? I told him that I was praying. He resounded, for 2 hours? And so I asked him, what's the problem?

I was told that I could only pray for 15 minutes. I laughed, because this was illegal. My prayers didn't violate any of the safety or security of the facility.

According to the first amendment, I could practice my religion without hinderance or penalty.

Then he threatens me, calls me boy, and said I better not do it again.

That next morning, early hours. Same old 2 step. Same cop popping shit, I gave him the same lyrics but I added, "if I only have 15 minutes to pray, please put this in writing. Then I'll have no choice but to comply, but until then, I'll be doing my prayers the way I've been."

I thought I saw smoke coming out of his ears. But later that day, he made good on his threats. I was called to the property room and told either I take my shades off and prepare to send them home right now or they get me reaffiliated and sent back to the gang block. I liked my shades, they were stylish.

I liked my medium security status better, and so, I took my luxury off my face and humbled myself. Also, they made me give up my blue thick thermal top and Kuffi's. I could live without these things but hated to be antagonized.

Every day, they were calling me down to the property room to take something else.

They did what I expected, which was to continue to abuse their authority and I kept on praying and striving to be a better man.

Even though at times the old foolish me wants to get crazy with these people and make them back off. I heard, "the best revenge is success."

"And by the will of God, this is how I'll repay them"
Allahhuakbar. God is the greatest.

38 CARL ROBINSON

After the warden of Brooklyn came through our block making her rounds, and I addressed the issue of harassment, 2 days later I was transferred.

So altogether I spent 6 days in Brooklyn CI. That was 6 days too many if you ask me. My new destination was Carl Robinson CI, in Enfield, CT.

This was only 15-20 minutes away from Hartford. I'm getting closer. As soon as I got off of the prison bus, I smelled gun powder. I really did. I could smell the streets of Hartford in the air. As crazy as that may sound, it's true.

After intake and medical cleared me, I was sent to 5 building. Which is the orientation building. You would usually stay there for 30 days tops, then move on to one of the other buildings.

Every building was a dorm. On the outside, it looked like a smurfs house. The inside looked like a refugee camp, shelter, or slave's warehouse.

Carl Robinson was an open compound. 3-4 buildings would go to the chow hall at once. A riot could possibly break out at any given time. The outside rec yard usually held about 700 people at once. This could've potentially been a deadly scene.

I knew a few people on the compound, but that didn't matter much to me. I got sent to 6 building. It wasn't bad. A few young dudes from Hartford was there, they hated my militance. I usually develop a routine surrounded by acts of faith, praying, studying, working out etc, and stick to it hard body.

Hartford cats usually stuck together when it benefitted and exchanged war stories. Mostly lies and ping ponged them through their cipher. I was never around for that. I'm a leader.

An older Muslim brother named Yaya moved to the block. He was in prison for 25 years, soon to be free. We talked every day, played a little chess, and spoke about his plans for the future.

We prayed together often. Sometimes, the young punks from Hartford would walk past us, but be way too close, considering we were only worshipping our lord. Our lord that created all things in existence, from above the heavens, to underneath the earths soil.

So how should that afford us courtesy, right? Well, these suckers these days don't respect much. Being a Muslim had me really checking myself first, then making a more clear observation of the world around me.

In order for things to get better, it had to start with me. I thank the most high for allowing me to see just how foolish and out of control my life has been.

Prison affected people. One way or the other, which is either you get better as a human being, mending your ways and prepared yourself to be an asset in society. Rarely, or you become scum. More violent, ignorant, self destructive, unaware, blinded and deluded of reality.

It's now or never for me. God has been sparing me from the ultimate destruction all my life. Chance after chance. Gift after gift. I will not squander this opportunity to get myself together.

Perfection is what I'll strive for, but will never achieve, but I will continue this journey, God willing, to becoming a better man. A better father, a good husband, a good son to my mother, a better brother, to my brothers and sisters.

A productive member of society, a good neighbor, a good businessman. Who knows, maybe even a mentor to the youth.

I am the oldest 6th grader, but the sky is the limit. Oh, and I got my Jacky back. God gave her back to me, she's riding. My families on deck, my kids are beautiful and brilliant. Parole shot me down.

That isn't changing my faith in the least. I'm sad, but I'll be alright, god willing. I'm healthy, confident, and determined to succeed. I must. I believe God has some beautiful things lined up for me.

As far as earth goes, I'll be there soon God willing. I'll be through your hood slanging this book, oils, lip gloss, body wash, weaves, etc. I'm grinding. Legitimately though, odds are against me, but I'll make it.

"I got God, and I got love. I'm good."

Made in the USA
Columbia, SC
18 June 2024

36909555R00095